Soups & Sides
for Every Season

a collection of soups, salads, breads, and desserts for
complete meals anytime

Alyce Morgan

Wine Pairings by Drew Robinson, CS

moretimeatthetable.com

Copyright © 2014

Moretimeatthetable Publishing

Colorado Springs, Colorado

A few recipes previously were published in full or in part on the author's blogs:

Moretimeatthetable.com

Dinnerplace.blogspot.com

Wine Pairings by Drew Robinson

Edited by Patricia Miller

Designed by Amanda Weber

Cover art by Daniel Craig

Manufactured in the United States of America

ISBN-13: 978-0615673066
ISBN-10: 0615673066

Soups & Sides
for Every Season

For *Dave, Sean, and Emily*--

Without whom I wouldn't have had a reason to cook.

Table of Contents

Breads and Spreads

Introduction

1

On any Saturday afternoon growing up, I might walk into the kitchen of our far-south-suburban Chicago house and, rolling my eyes in fear, say, "What's in that pot?" My dad, a farm boy born and raised in southern Louisiana and married during the Depression, was a cook born out of love and necessity. If there was anything he couldn't or didn't cook, I don't know what it was. And if there was a soup he didn't throw together, I have yet to hear of it. His vegetable soup, pronounced "wejtable," was legendary, but, of course, he had a vegetable garden fit for a king on that acre of land adjacent to the pond we skated on all winter. Why wouldn't wejtable soup be to die for made with God's own ingredients right from the yard? In case you think we (and there were two sisters and a brother rolling their eyes right along with me) were always happy to find that cauldron going, let me set you straight. Because Dad considered anything living —but hopefully, but not always, dead when he brought it home — fair game for the table, we truly never knew what might be in that pot. He also hunted and fished, despite the fact that he made a fair salary working for the railroad. I guess we were the original locavores.

Fast-forward through life — years of cooking for a growing family and friends in several states and even Europe — and you have a veteran food blogger who finally decided to write a cookbook. When good friends suggested a book with easier recipes and my own computer index showing a plethora of soups, I began to test and taste, bringing almost everyone I knew along with me into the soup pot. In the year of developing and testing recipes, I can honestly say I never got tired of eating soup or the wonderful breads and salads that can make soup a meal for a big family or company. That tells you a lot about these glorious and ever-changeable kettles of goodness.

If this is your first foray into soup making, you'll find being a soup cook is great fun. Soup is flexible. It's usually healthy, often inexpensive and uses up pesky leftovers beautifully. It's easy to share with friends, along with a glass of wine, some bread and cheese, and a small dessert. Extra soup? Store it in freezer containers. Need lunches for work? Soup is simple and filling. Just ladle a few servings into individual containers for the week. Tired of your own soup repertoire? Invite a few friends to each make a pot and set up a soup swap.

And while I promise you can identify every single ingredient in the pots of soup you'll love creating and sharing from this book, I'm not sure I'll ever live up to Dad's wejtable. But I'll keep trying.

--Alyce Morgan

Saint Paul, Minnesota, and Colorado Springs, Colorado
October 2013

About this Book

My soups are just the kind of meals I put on the table day and night, many times paired with a slice of baguette and a piece of cheese or a salad. They're often made with what's in the fridge, on the counter or left on the back porch by a gardening neighbor. This little book — full of fun, well-tested soups and the sides to go with them — is meant to help you to create delicious meals. Partnering a warm or cold bowl of soup with a lovely glass of wine chosen by Drew Robinson, CS, and perhaps a salad — or even a dessert— will fill your tummy happily and thriftily. These recipes and ideas may provide you lunch for the next few days, a freezer meal for a busy weeknight, or a meal to take to a friend. Throughout the book, dishes with an * indicate these are recipes from the book.

My friends and family know they may walk in for dinner and find a stack of soup bowls on the kitchen counter, a big pot bubbling away on the stove, and wine and glasses set out in the dining room. Because I enjoy this help-yourself kind of entertaining, there are ideas for impromptu gatherings so you'll feel free to send an email or text mid-afternoon: I've got a pot of soup on. Can you bring bread? No big kitchen work-out or empty wallet to worry about; a pot of soup and a good loaf of bread make most people happy, full and loved. The point is to be together and soup makes that easy, healthy, inexpensive and fun. And cleanup means stacking rinsed bowls and an empty pot in the sink for the morning.

My friend and fellow cook, writer Lani Jordan, encouraged me to write a book for today's cooks — with methods or recipes that often could be done in half an hour. While some of these soups require more time, many (especially after you've made them once) are done in no time. There you are, Lani!

So keep your pantry, larder and fridge stocked with things like broth, onions, carrots, celery, fresh parsley, noodles, rice, canned tomatoes, beans and a few bottles of wine. In your freezer make sure there are ham hocks, a package of boneless chicken thighs or shrimp. Buy some great bowls and dishwasher-safe wine glasses. Then you won't be too far away from feeding whoever comes through the door. And isn't that what cooking is all about?

More on Soup

For a complete guide to soup making:

The New Book of Soups
by The Culinary Institute of America,
Lebhar-Friedman, 2009.

For a history of soup:

Soup Through the Ages: A Culinary History With Recipes by Victoria R. Rumble, McFarland, 2009

For another small soup
book with photos:

Sunday Soups by Betty Rosbottom and Charles Schiller,
Chronicle Books, 2008.

For recipes online:

Use trusted sources such as finecooking.com, nytimes.com, Americastestkitchen.com (I test for them.) and epicurious.com.

Blogs:

Naturally I recommend my own blogs for soup and more: moretimeatthetable.com and dinnerplace.blogspot.com.

For an all-soup blog, visit Rhode Island food writer Lydia Walshin's take on soups at soupchick.com.

Soups for Autumn

If you live where the seasons truly change, and you love to cook, you're happy when the temperature drops and a cold wind blows in the first fall soup day. Perfectly suited to cooler weather, these soups will say good-bye to summer and usher in the time of kicking dry leaves, tailgates, Halloween parties, and Thanksgiving.

Many of them take advantage of the last of the farmer's market goodies and combine them with the longer-lasting vegetables such as carrots and winter squash. There are hearty stews like Mexican Posole and Tuscan Chicken Stew that are suitable for families or parties, as well as an easy-to-follow method for making use of that Thanksgiving turkey carcass to make a top-shelf Turkey Noodle Soup. Parmesan-Peanut Spicy Pumpkin, Two-Mushroom Soup with Cheddar, and Creamy Butternut Squash Soup are easily made vegetarian or vegan by replacing chicken stock with vegetable stock and/or by omitting dairy.

Spicy Red Lentil Soup
with Cucumber-Feta-Cilantro Salsa

serves 6-8

In the Mac-Groveland neighborhood of Saint Paul, right on Grand Avenue, we have a small and always full middle-Eastern restaurant called Shish. It's the gathering place for great coffee, inexpensive and luscious breakfasts, vegetarian or lamb lunches, foot-tall layer cakes, and even cookies. A staple on Shish's vegetarian menu is its Red Lentil Soup. While mine isn't a whole lot like their famous version, it takes its inspiration from the summer I took music grad classes at nearby University of St. Thomas, sitting at Shish's café tables enjoying a bowl. Easily made vegan with a change to vegetable broth and leaving off the feta, this is also a quicker lentil soup, since red lentils cook so much faster than their green or brown relatives. The bright, addictive flavors of ginger and curry made Spicy Red Lentil the favorite of everyone who tested it, including children.

2 cups red lentils

8 cups (64 ounces) chicken or vegetable broth

1 15-ounce can chopped tomatoes

2 tablespoons olive oil

2 tablespoons fresh ginger, minced

2 cloves garlic, minced

1/2 teaspoon freshly ground black pepper

Generous pinch crushed red pepper

2 teaspoons curry powder

1 teaspoon ground cumin

2 *each* onions, carrots, celery, cut into 1/2-inch dice

1 teaspoon kosher salt

1/2 cup white wine

3 tablespoons tomato paste

Salsa:

1/2 cup each feta cheese, chopped cucumber and chopped cilantro

1 Rinse lentils thoroughly in a colander several times. Set aside.

2 Pour the broth into a 4-6-quart pan and heat over high until boiling; lower heat to a simmer. You also can heat the broth in the microwave if you have a microwave-safe casserole or pot large enough. I use my 8-cup Pyrex measuring cup.

3 In an 8-quart pot, heat olive oil over low heat with ginger, garlic, curry powder, black pepper and crushed red pepper. Cook, stirring, 1-2 minutes.

4 Raise heat to medium. Add diced vegetables and salt; stir well. Cover and let cook, stirring once, for 2 minutes.

5 Raise heat and add wine; let cook 1 minute, stirring. Add lentils and stir well.

6 Add tomato paste and hot broth mixture. Bring to a boil and cover. Cook until lentils are tender, about 15 minutes. Taste and adjust seasonings. While soup is cooking, combine the salsa ingredients and set aside. This soup is attractive as is, somewhat chunky in texture, but you can puree part or all of the soup in batches in a food processor or blender or, if you have an immersion blender, right in the pot. Serve hot, garnished with salsa.

Make it a Meal

Accompaniments:

Grilled pita bread with hummus.

Wine:

Spicy, yet rich. A Gewurztraminer or maybe Viognier, if you can get one without too much oak in it.

Dessert:

Fresh fruit (apples would be lovely) with a small scoop of plain yogurt and a drizzle of honey.

Two Mushroom Red Onion Soup
with Cheddar

serves 6-8

A really quick warm-up for a cold fall day or an easy first course for a special dinner, this healthy soup is full of inexpensive and easily found ingredients that come together by the time you've set the table and poured drinks. If you have a little more time, rehydrate one ounce dried chanterelle mushrooms and add both the chopped mushrooms and strained broth for a three-mushroom soup. Your farmers' market — or friends who are mushroom hunters — might have other fresh, local mushrooms. In that case, use those. A crusty loaf of bread is a necessary side; there's a lot of dunking to be done here. Top with a teaspoon of grated Cheddar to bring all the flavors together.

1 tablespoon butter

2 tablespoons olive oil

1 medium red onion, cut into 1/8s

2 cloves garlic, sliced

1 carrot, peeled, trimmed, and cut into 2-inch pieces

1 stalk celery, cut into 2-inch pieces

1/2 teaspoon each kosher salt and fresh-ground black pepper

2 teaspoons fresh thyme, chopped (or 1 teaspoon dried thyme), plus 2 sprigs thyme

1/8 teaspoon crushed red pepper

8 ounces button mushrooms, sliced

4 ounces shitake mushrooms, sliced

1/2 cup white wine

5 cups chicken or vegetable broth

1/2 cup grated Cheddar cheese for garnish

1 Heat the butter and one tablespoon of the olive oil in an 8-quart pot over medium heat. Meanwhile, chop the onion, garlic, carrot, and celery finely in the food proccessor or by hand, and add to the pot.

2 Season vegetables with salt, pepper and half of the fresh or dried thyme. Let cook 5 minutes or so, stirring occasionally, until vegetables begin to soften. Add white wine, stir for 1 minute and add stock. Bring to a boil; lower heat to a simmer.

3 In a large skillet, heat the other tablespoon of olive oil over medium-high heat with the crushed red pepper. Sauté about 1/2 cup of mushrooms at a time, removing cooked mushrooms to a bowl, and adding more to the skillet. When all of the mushrooms are browned, add them to the broth mixture.

4 Let soup simmer another 5 minutes or so. Serve hot, garnishing with the thyme sprigs and pass the grated cheese at the table.

Make it a Meal

Accompaniments:

Any crusty bread such as baguette or a sourdough boule.

Wine:

A lighter red would be perfect here; Cabernet and Zin will overwhelm it. On a budget, New Zealand Pinot Noir jumps out. Special occasion, try a single-vineyard Pinot Noir from Oregon, or the best Burgundy you can afford. Earthiness goes with the 'shrooms; Oregon will give you a bit more fruit than the French (Burgundy.)

Dessert:

Pears poached in red wine or port

Creamy Butternut and Other Squash Soup

serves 6-8

This soup is not the time-consuming, but popular, Butternut Squash we're used to come fall. Instead, it's a one-two punch meal, light and quick, but nutritious and perfect for dinner with an interesting cheese and bread. Of course it could also serve as a colorful first course for Thanksgiving if you like. Like many soups, this one is almost better warmed up in the microwave the next day. It uses the rest of late summer's zucchini or yellow squash, as well as the winter squash you couldn't resist at the market. Freeze a bowl or two — there's nothing like food in reserve to make you feel rich. If you have a friend who's not feeling well, this makes a lovely comfort soup.

2 tablespoons olive oil

1 cup each chopped onion and celery

1 each: small-medium zucchini and yellow (summer) squash, unpeeled, diced

1/2 cup chopped carrot

2 cloves garlic, minced

Kosher salt and fresh-ground black pepper

Pinch of crushed red pepper

2 tablespoons fresh thyme, or 1 1/2 teaspoons dried thyme

1/2 cup chopped fresh parsley

1/4 teaspoon ground ginger, optional

2 -3 cups butternut squash, chopped and peeled

8 cups (64-ounces) chicken or vegetable stock

1/2 cup plain Greek yogurt, optional, or 1/4 cup grated Parmesan cheese, for garnish

1 To an 8-10-quart pot, add olive oil and sauté onion, celery, zucchini, yellow squash, and carrots over medium-high heat until softened. Add garlic and season with 1/2 teaspoon salt and 1/4 teaspoon fresh ground black pepper. Stir in crushed red pepper, 1/2 of the thyme, parsley and ginger.

2 Stir in butternut squash and cook a few minutes, stirring. Add stock, stir well, and bring to a boil. Reduce heat and simmer until vegetables are tender, 15-20 minutes.

3 Taste, and adjust seasoning. If desired, puree the soup in batches in a food processor, blender or if you have an immersion blender, right in the pot. If the soup is too thick, add a little more water or stock. If too thin, simmer a few minutes more until reduced and thickened.

4 Ladle into bowls and garnish with thyme and a spoonful of Greek yogurt or a sprinkle of Parmesan. Serve hot.

Make it a Meal

Accompaniments:

Tuna Quesadillas* or Tuna-Cannellini Bean Salad with Feta*

Wine:

Let's match, rather than contrast, this soup with one of several options: Viognier, a less-sweet sherry like Amontillado, rich (but not oaky) Chardonnay, and last, Meursault or Puligny Montrachet. Think richness on the palate, but not tons of vanilla from oak.

Dessert:

Individual Kiwi Tarts* or Maple Syrup Brown Rice Pudding*

Tuscan Chicken Stew

serves 6-8

I have always thought of chicken minestrone soup — the inspiration for this stew — as one of the healthiest and most delicious of the whole-meal soups. My original version is for a lazy Sunday afternoon or the lucky person who stays in from skiing and gets to spend the day making dinner. This abbreviated recipe compresses a day's soup making into a much shorter time by using boneless chicken thighs and canned beans. If you'd rather use homemade beans, make your own overnight in the slow cooker or freeze two cups or so when you've made a pot of beans. If you're concerned about fat, leave out the bacon and use olive oil. The soup will still be delectable.

2 strips bacon, cut into 1/2-inch pieces or 2 tablespoons olive oil

1/8 teaspoon crushed red pepper

2 onions, chopped

3 each: carrots, peeled and trimmed, and celery stalks with leaves, chopped

4 garlic cloves, minced

1/2 cup chopped fresh parsley

2 tablespoons fresh rosemary, minced or 1 tablespoon dried rosemary, crumbled

1/2 teaspoon *each*: dried basil and oregano

Kosher salt and fresh-ground black pepper

6 boneless, skinless chicken thighs, cut into 1-inch pieces

1/4 cup white wine

1 15-ounce can chopped tomatoes

1 15-ounce can cannellini (or Great Northern) beans, rinsed and drained

4 cups low-sodium chicken stock

1 cup fresh zucchini, cut into 1/2-inch pieces

1 cup fresh spinach, coarsely chopped

1/2 cup grated Parmesan cheese, for garnish

1 In a large soup pot, fry bacon over medium heat until crispy. Remove bacon to a plate lined with paper towel, leaving bacon fat in the pot. If not using bacon, heat the olive oil with the crushed red pepper. Sprinkle in the crushed red pepper and let cook 30 seconds or so.

2 Add the onions, carrots and celery to the fat. Cover, and cook about 3 minutes; add garlic. Stir in parsley, rosemary, basil, oregano and season with 1/2 teaspoon kosher salt and 1/4 teaspoon fresh-ground black pepper.
Cook 1 minute.

3 In a medium bowl, toss the cut-up chicken pieces with a sprinkle of salt and pepper; add to the pot, stirring well so the chicken pieces are at the bottom. Cook, stirring, until chicken is browned, about 5 minutes.

4 Pour in white wine and stir well to bring up the browned bits at the bottom of the pot. Cook 1 minute or so; add tomatoes, beans and chicken stock.
Stir well.

5 Bring to a boil, reduce heat, and let soup simmer until vegetables are tender and chicken is cooked through, with no pink at the center.

6 Stir in zucchini, spinach and reserved bacon, and simmer another 2 minutes or so until zucchini is nearly tender and spinach is wilted. Taste and adjust seasonings.

7 Serve hot with grated Parmesan cheese.

Make it a Meal

Accompaniments:

Toasted Almond-Broccolini Salad*. Garlic bread or any crusty loaf.

Wine:

A lighter Italian red like a less-expensive Chianti (no wicker baskets — called a "fiasco" in Italian, and for good reason). No need for a Chianti Classico Reserva; it would likely be too tanic and dark for this soup. Special occasion: best Chianti Classico you can find.

Dessert:

Spumoni ice cream or cannelloni from the Italian bakery.

Cook's Notes:

You can add a 1/4 cup tiny pasta, such as tubetti or ditalini, once the soup is boiling. If you have it, throw in a rind from Parmesan cheese. (I save them in the freezer for such use.) Other or leftover vegetables (green beans, yellow squash, green peas, etc.)? Toss them in.

Pork Tenderloin Posole

serves 6-8

This is a fast, spicy version of the famous old Mexican stew typically made with pork butt. Other versions use chicken or no meat at all. Even better the next day, this soup is richly filling and makes a whole meal with very little effort. Be sure you buy the toppings (radishes, onions, etc.) because the crunch on top makes the dish. A hearty meal anytime, I think it's perfect for football tailgating, Super Bowl parties, the Saturday after Thanksgiving or after Christmas Eve service.

4 tablespoons olive oil

2 onions, cut into 1/8s

2 medium carrots, cut into 1-inch pieces

2 celery stalks, cut into 1-inch pieces

1 tablespoon chili powder

1 teaspoon ground cumin

1 tablespoon dried oregano

1 teaspoon kosher salt

1/2 teaspoon fresh- ground black pepper

1/2 teaspoon crushed red pepper

2 cloves garlic, minced

1 pound pork tenderloin, sliced into 1-inch-thick coins, then quarter each coin

15-ounce can chopped tomatoes

2 4-ounce cans chopped mild green chiles, drained

4 cups low-sodium chicken broth

29-ounce can hominy, rinsed and drained

2 cups corn, fresh or frozen

Toppings: 3 sliced limes, 1 bunch sliced radishes, 1 cup chopped onions or green onions, 1 cup shredded lettuce, 2 sliced avocadoes and/or 2 cups grated Cheddar or Monterey Jack cheese

1 Heat 2 tablespoons olive oil in a 6- or 8-quart stockpot over low heat. Finely chop onions, carrots and celery in a food processor or by hand. Add the vegetables to the stockpot and season with chili powder, cumin, oregano, 1/2 teaspoon kosher salt, 1/2 teaspoon fresh-ground black pepper and 1/4 teaspoon crushed red pepper. Stir well; raise heat to medium and cover. Cook 5 minutes, stirring regularly; add garlic during the last minute of cooking.

2 Heat a large skillet over high heat and add the other 2 tablespoons of olive oil. In a medium bowl, toss the cut-up pork tenderloin with 1/4 teaspoon salt and 1/4 teaspoon crushed red pepper. Add to skillet, turning so nicely browned on all sides; turn off heat under the skillet and add the pork to the stockpot, scraping any juices and browned bits into the pot.

3 Stir in tomatoes, chiles, broth, hominy and corn on top of the pork; bring to a rolling boil. Lower heat a bit, and cook for just a few more minutes until hominy and corn are hot and the posole has thickened slightly. Serve hot with garnishes in bowls on the table.

Make it a Meal

Accompaniments:

1 dozen warmed tortillas

Wine:

A Malbec or Syrah or, on a budget, a Cotes du Rhone Villages. Special occasion, a Northern Rhone like Cote Rotie. If you choose an Australian Shiraz, make sure the wine is from a cooler sub-region like Adelaide Hills or Coonawarra. Tannic reds will turn bitter, so skip them.

Other Drinks:

A Mexican beer like Corona or Dos Equis or iced tea

Dessert:

Cinnamon ice cream or flan

Parmesan-Peanut Spicy Pumpkin Soup

6 first-course
or
4 main-course
servings

I've made a number of pumpkin soups over the years. It's a tasty Halloween-night supper, and it will enchant your guests when served in beautiful tiny bowls or cups as a first course at Thanksgiving. Pumpkin soup, if not too spicy, makes a healing gift to take to a sick friend or make it in a slow cooker to share with co-workers for a fall potluck or work lunch. This version takes the best of my pumpkin soups and puts them together for a fast, nutritious meal. My next-door neighbor happily grows and shares the gorgeous thyme and sage that inspired this soup. I dedicate my recipe to the best front-yard vegetable gardener in Saint Paul. She knows who she is.

1 tablespoon butter

1 garlic clove, minced

1 medium red onion, cut into eighths

1 stalk celery, trimmed, and cut into 1-inch pieces

1 carrot, peeled, trimmed, and cut into 1-inch pieces

4 fresh sage leaves or 1 teaspoon dried sage, rubbed

2 teaspoons fresh thyme, chopped or 3/4 teaspoon dried thyme

1/2 teaspoon kosher salt

1/4 teaspoon fresh-ground pepper

3-5 drops hot sauce

15-ounce can 100% pumpkin (not pumpkin pie filling)

2 teaspoons peanut butter

4 cups (1 quart) low-sodium chicken stock

1/2 cup heavy cream or non-fat evaporated milk, optional

1/3 cup *each* grated Parmesan cheese and chopped peanuts, for garnish

1 In a 4-6 quart pot, heat butter with garlic over medium low heat.

2 Finely chop by hand or in a food processor onions, celery, carrot, sage and thyme. Add vegetable-herb mixture to the pot and stir; season with salt, pepper and hot sauce, stirring well.

3 Stir in pumpkin, peanut butter and chicken stock. Bring to a boil, stirring.

4 Reduce heat, cover and simmer 10 minutes. If using cream or milk, stir in now, and warm through 1-2 minutes without boiling. Taste and adjust seasonings.

5 Serve in warm bowls, passing cheese, peanuts and black pepper at the table.

Cook's Notes: This soup doubles easily

Make it a Meal

Accompaniments:

My Greens with Lemon Vinaigrette and Cheese Toast* is luscious here, but this is also a fine meal on its own with biscuits or cheese and fruit. If served for Thanksgiving, it's delish with a grilled turkey sandwich the next day.

Wine:

Perfect for whiff-of-pepper Gewurztraminer (Alsace, Austria or Germany), which loves any food with spice! Dry Riesling would work as well, but not a good pairing for a super-sweet $6 Riesling. Special occasion, I'm a sucker for a great Alsatian Riesling or Gewurztraminer.

Dessert:

Hot tea and tiny butter cookies for dunking. If you want a larger dessert, any apple cake or one of my Individual Kiwi Tarts* would work.

Lamb-Italian Sausage Stew

serves 6-8

In our house in Colorado Springs, the kitchen is two steps up from the sunroom, where I often work at the table, but also have a small television. Many days I've left a program on to listen to while I cooked or cleaned up in the kitchen. Sometimes I paid more attention than others. One day, Emeril Lagasse was making a stew with lamb and Italian sausage and beans; that was about all I heard. I didn't remember any other ingredients or the cooking method, but another day, with those three ingredients in mind, I decided to make a lamb stew in the slow cooker and have been making it ever since.

A hearty meal for the family that could cook all day while you're skiing, this stew also could be stretched to feed 10 guests, if served over rice or egg noodles. Cooking it on top of the stove works quite well, but you'll need two or more additional cups of broth or water, since it cooks down.

2 tablespoons olive oil

2 pounds lamb (boneless leg, shoulder, or stew meat), cut into 1-2-inch pieces

Kosher salt and fresh-ground black pepper

1 pound hot Italian sausage links (4-5 pieces), cut into 1-2-inch pieces

2 medium-large onions, chopped

2 stalks celery, chopped

3 cloves garlic, minced

1 teaspoon *each* fresh rosemary and thyme, chopped or 1/2 teaspoon *each* dry

6 cups low-sodium beef broth

1 cup red wine

32-ounce can chopped tomatoes

4 cups cooked white beans

1 In a large bowl, toss lamb with 1/4 teaspoon each salt and pepper. In a large skillet, heat oil over medium heat. Add lamb and Italian sausage and cook until well-browned, about 10 minutes.

2 Add onions, celery, garlic, rosemary and thyme. Sprinkle with a pinch each of salt and pepper. Cook 5-7 minutes until vegetables are softened.

3 Add meat mixture to a 6-quart slow cooker. Pour in beef broth, wine and tomatoes; stir in drained beans. Cook on low 6-8 hours. Taste and adjust seasonings.

Stovetop directions:

Follow directions above, but cook meat, vegetables, and herbs in an 8-quart pot with a lid. Add broth, tomatoes and wine, along with an additional 2 cups water or broth. Bring to a boil; reduce to a simmer. Cook until lamb is tender, about 1 1/2 hours. Stir in cooked beans and simmer 10-15 minutes. Taste, and adjust seasonings.

Cook's Notes:

You may use 2-3 cans any variety of white beans, drained, or you may cook your own beans. If cooking your own beans, they don't need to be completely done when you add them; they'll cook more with the stew. I like beans cooked in a microwave — they cook through without breaking apart, peeling or becoming mushy. You also can cook them on the stove.

Microwave directions: In a large, microwave-safe bowl, combine 2 cups dry white beans, picked over and rinsed, 4 cups water, 1 large onion, halved and with the skin on, 4 cloves garlic with papers, 3 sprigs fresh rosemary or 1 teaspoon dried and 1 teaspoon freshly ground pepper. Microwave at full-power for about 35 minutes or until tender. Drain beans, remove vegetables and herbs. Season with 1/4 teaspoon salt.

Stovetop directions: Place all ingredients in a 4-quart pan with cover. Add more water until beans are covered by about 4 inches of liquid. Bring to a boil. Reduce heat to a simmer and cook until beans are tender, 1-1 1/2 hours, checking occasionally to make sure there is enough liquid in the pot for the beans to boil freely. Drain, removing vegetables and herbs. Season with 1/4 teaspoon salt.

Make it a Meal

Accompaniments:

Crusty bread, such as baguette or boule, with a green salad

Wine:

A hearty red here, and nothing goes better with lamb than Bordeaux! On a budget, a Cabernet (or Cabernet blend) from Sonoma, rather than from Napa; it's more food friendly. Special occasion, go for the best Bordeaux you can afford. Stay away from generic wine that just says Bordeaux, Bordeaux Superiore or Medoc on the label. Get a wine from a specific sub-region, such as Pauillac, Margaux or St. Estephe. These will be Cabernet-based wines, but Merlot-based wines from Pomerol and St. Emilion will be very good as well

Dessert:

Sorbet or a cheese tray, along with some small, excellent chocolates.

Turkey Noodle Soup
from Thanksgiving Leftovers

10+ quarts
of soup

Save your turkey carcass well-wrapped in the freezer for up to two months, and you have the makings of a wonderful turkey noodle soup later on. If you want to make the soup within two days or so of your Thanksgiving feast, you have the option of using leftovers and probably will end up with a wonderful soup, even without the carcass.

While not terribly quick to make — about an hour and half — there's nothing really difficult about the process, and this soup is: 1. delicious and 2. can be frozen once made and cooled. The soup is made in two stages: making the stock and making the soup. If you are short of time and storage space, you might make the stock in the slow cooker Thanksgiving night. You'll then be ready to start the soup the next day.

Making the stock:

Turkey carcass plus extra bits of turkey meat, gristle, or skin

1 large onion, skin on, well washed and cut in half

2 carrots, whole, unpeeled

2 stalks celery with leaves, cut in half (put the end of the celery in, too, if you have it)

1 bay leaf

Handful of fresh parsley (no need to chop)

1 tablespoon whole peppercorns

2 teaspoons kosher salt

1 Place all the ingredients into a large stockpot; 12 quarts is plenty, although a larger pot might be helpful. Add enough water to cover the carcass and vegetables; cover and cook over high heat. Bring to a rolling boil, then reduce the heat to a medium boil, and let cook an hour or so with the lid ajar to prevent boil-overs. Add more water to keep all ingredients covered.

2 Strain the stock and ingredients through a large colander; discard all solids. You also can fish out the very soft vegetables, puree them and add back into the plain stock. Be careful to make sure you have all of the peppercorns out of the stock. You now have the basis for your soup.

Making the soup:

1   cup chopped onion

2   cups chopped celery

4   cloves garlic, minced

6   large carrots, peeled, and
     cut into 1-inch pieces

1   cup chopped fresh parsley

3   tablespoons each chopped
     fresh thyme and sage (or 1
     teaspoon each dry)

2-3 cups leftover
      Thanksgiving vegetables,
      whole or pureed, or
      pureed or 2-3 cups frozen/
      fresh vegetables

1-2 cups leftover
      Thanksgiving gravy

2   cups (or more) leftover
     chopped or shredded
     turkey, light or dark meat

2-4 quarts turkey stock or
      low-sodium chicken broth,
      plus any turkey stock
      that's left

1   24-ounce package fresh,
     frozen noodles

1   cup frozen peas

Kosher salt and fresh ground
     pepper, to taste

3-4 drops hot sauce, or
      to taste

Cook's Notes:

If you don't have a turkey carcass, use several quarts canned chicken or turkey broth to cover the vegetables and follow the rest of the directions.

If you have cruciferous vegetables such as broccoli, cabbage or cauliflower, chop and add them with the frozen peas. If you add them earlier, they'll lend their strong flavors to the broth and that's not what you want. Good choices for vegetables are: green beans, asparagus, zucchini, onions, potatoes, sweet potatoes, parsnips, turnips, etc. Even mashed potatoes or creamed onions can be added, especially if they'll go to waste otherwise. Vegetables like mashed sweet potatoes are best left to their own devices and eaten separately.

Make it a Meal

Accompaniments:

This soup is pretty much a complete meal. A small dish of cranberry relish from Thanksgiving dinner might be nice.

Wine:

In case you have any leftover wine from Turkey Fest, and you liked it, I would stick with that. If starting anew, keep it light, but not too oaky. Your favorite middle-of- the-road California Chardonnay, Italian Pinot Grigio, or for the more special occasion, an Oregon Chardonnay, would all be good pairings.

Dessert:

I hope you have some leftover pie, but if not, my Pumpkin Custard with Cinnamon Crème Fraîche* would be perfect.

1 Add all of the ingredients, except for noodles, peas, salt and pepper and hot sauce, to the pot of stock. You may need to add water, broth or stock until the vegetables are able to float freely. The broth will reduce during cooking, and you'll need quite a bit for boiling the noodles.

2 Bring to a rolling boil and lower heat to a good simmer. Cook until the fresh vegetables begin to soften, stirring regularly.

3 When the vegetables are soft, add the frozen noodles and cook in the broth according to the package instructions, about 20 minutes. If you're using dried noodles, cooking time will be less. Throw in the peas during the last few minutes. Add salt, pepper and hot sauce; taste and adjust seasonings. A few drops of hot sauce will deepen the flavor of the soup without making it hot, but be careful not to overdo it. Total cooking time may be 30-40 minutes.

Serve soup hot. Cool and cover any leftovers and refrigerate for a day. Or freeze the soup in freezer containers for up to 6 months.

Soups for Winter

I am seldom happier than when I wake on a winter morning to see a blanket of white across my garden. Even though my children are long since out of school, I still turn on the news to hear the weather and about school closings. If the buses aren't running or the anchorperson is insisting we not go out unless it's an emergency, I feel absolutely free as a bird, even though I might not have been going out anyway. Snow day! Can't go to work, can't go to the store. Guess I'll have to whip up a big pot of soup that will simmer on the back burner and fill the house with wafting love. In fact, I usually keep a few things in the freezer and pantry for times like this; I *plan* on being stuck. I pray for it, in fact. I might even make bread, too!

Several of these soups are perfect for a snow day with no chance for a grocery run — 3-Bean Bacon with Kale or Lemon Split Pea with Peppered Sour Cream — but others are just as luscious and wonderful although they require a bit more planning. There are vegan or vegetarian options for several of the soups, and while I'm not a vegan, I include my own favorite spicy Vegan Chili with Cilantro Rice.

While soup is a nutritious, healthy, inexpensive, and simple meal anytime of the year, it does lend itself to winter when all we want to do is stay warm. If you're the cook for your skiing, skating or snowmobiling group, you're in luck here; the Turkey-Wild Rice with Vegetables and Sherry will stick with the smiling crew and make them all full and content. The Next-Day Pot Roast Soup takes care of the leftovers from a pot roast supper and provides a pretty effortless lunch. Whichever soup you choose — and I hope you try all of them — you'll feel rich, coddled and well-fed by the time the meal's over.

3 Bean-Bacon with Kale

serves 6

This hearty, but fresh-tasting soup just about makes itself and is the perfect reason for keeping a well-filled pantry. A few chopped vegetables, some dried herbs, canned beans, broth, tomatoes — and you have your meal. Grate some Parmesan cheese for garnish. You can easily adapt it to a vegan soup.

- 2 slices bacon, chopped into 1/2-inch pieces
- 2 onions, cut into small dice
- 3 carrots, cut into small dice
- 3 stalks celery, chopped finely
- 3 garlic cloves, minced
- 3/4 teaspoon kosher salt
- 1/2 teaspoon fresh-ground pepper
- 2 tablespoons Herbes de Provence (or mix of dried basil, rosemary and oregano)

- 15-ounce can chopped tomatoes
- 1 *each* (15-ounce) can white beans, black beans and garbanzo beans, rinsed and drained
- 1 cup kale, finely chopped
- 4 cups (32 ounces) low-sodium chicken broth
- A few drops hot sauce, optional
- 1/2 cup water
- 1/2 cup grated Parmesan cheese for garnish

Cook's Notes:

You can substitute spinach for the kale. Also, instead of the bacon, use one tablespoon olive oil and about 1/3 cup chopped ham. Chopping the onions, celery and carrots in a food processor will speed up the prep. For a vegan option, skip the bacon, use 2 tablespoons olive oil for cooking the vegetables and vegetable broth in place of the chicken broth.

1 Heat a heavy 6-8-quart pot over medium heat and add chopped bacon. Cook until just barely done. Pour or spoon out some of the bacon fat, leaving about 1 tablespoon in pot. Stir together the vegetables and bacon. Sprinkle with salt, pepper and dried herbs. Cover and cook 3-4 minutes, stirring occasionally.

2 Add tomatoes, beans, kale, broth, hot sauce (if using) and water. Bring to a boil. Reduce heat and cook until vegetables are nearly tender and soup has thickened a bit. Taste, and adjust seasonings.

3 Serve hot topped with grated Parmesan.

Make it a Meal

Accompaniments:

Cilantro Coleslaw*, toasted garlic bread or plain Italian bread for dunking.

Wine:

One of the great wines of the world: Nebbiolo. Not in your price range? Try a Dolcetto. Special occasion: something from the regions of Barbaresco or Barolo, both Nebbiolo-based and almost bullet-proof in terms of finding good producers.

Dessert:

Baked apples and Cheddar cheese.

Tomato Soup with *Fried Cheese*

serves 6

While tomato soup often waits for grilled cheese like Romeo waited for Juliet, this neat riff on the combination eliminates the bread while keeping the luscious melted cheese. First a quick tomato soup is stirred together in about 25 minutes. Then a piece of cheese is melted with a little olive oil in a small skillet. Ladle the soup, scrape the crispy-gooey cheese on top, and you're ready to eat.

8 tablespoons olive oil, divided

1 large onion, minced

2 peeled carrots, minced

1 cup fresh parsley, minced

3 garlic cloves, minced

Juice and grated peel of 1/2 lemon

1 28-ounce can chopped tomatoes

1 cup white wine or water

2 teaspoons honey

1 teaspoon sea salt

1/2 teaspoon fresh-ground white pepper

1/2 teaspoon chili-garlic sauce or a few drops of hot sauce

6 slices low-sodium Swiss or Cheddar cheese

Cook's Notes:

If you have a food processor, use it to speed up the prep by finely chopping the onions, celery, carrots, parsley, garlic and the half lemon.

1 In an 8-quart pot, warm 2 tablespoons of the olive oil for 1 minute over medium heat. Scoop in the minced vegetables, and cook about 5 minutes or until they begin to soften.

2 Add the remaining ingredients, except cheese, and bring to a boil. Lower heat to a simmer and cook slowly about 20 minutes, stirring regularly. If desired, puree part or all of the soup in batches in the food processor, blender or, if you have an immersion blender, right in the pot. Taste and adjust seasonings. Keep soup warm while you make the cheese.

3 For each serving, heat 1 tablespoon olive oil over medium heat in a small skillet. Add a slice of cheese and, watching closely, melt well. Ladle soup into a soup bowl. Scrape the melted cheese into the bowl and put the skillet back on the heat briefly. Scrape the now-crispy leavings of the cheese into the bowl. Repeat for each serving. Serve hot.

Make it a Meal

Accompaniments:

Whole-wheat soda crackers and a green salad with Alyce's Balsamic Vinaigrette*

Wine:

Daily: Chianti or Rosé. Special occasion: Beaujolais — not the Nouveau that comes out in November, which tastes like grape and banana bubble gum. Get one from one of the best 10 Crus of Beaujolais, from a sub-region such as Morgon or Moulin au Vent.

Dessert:

Individual Chocolate Microwaved Pudding Cakes*

Roasted Vegetable Soup

I often make a crusty pork loin roast and oven-roasted root vegetables in the cold seasons. It feeds a bunch of people easily, makes a stunning centerpiece and is a wonderful reason to pull out my best Pinot Noirs. One day I over-estimated the amount of vegetables we'd eat, and the leftovers became the next night's soup. Full of richly flavorful herbs combined with beautiful late-harvest vegetables, this soup makes me want fall to arrive quickly so I can make it then — and all winter long. Try the version made with left-over vegetables or make this soup from scratch by roasting the vegetables first. The crispy bacon garnish provides a nice crunch to complement the vegetables, or you can grill baguette slices for croutons.

1 sweet potato, peeled

1 butternut squash (1-1 1/2 pounds), peeled

1 turnip, peeled

1 medium potato, peeled

3 carrots, peeled

2 parsnips, peeled

2 tablespoons olive oil

2 cloves garlic, minced

2 teaspoons kosher salt

1 teaspoon freshly-ground pepper

2 medium onions, diced

1 cup celery, diced

2 tablespoons butter

8 cups (64 ounces) low-sodium chicken broth

1/2 cup fresh parsley, coarsely chopped

2 sprigs *each* fresh rosemary, thyme and sage or 1 teaspoon *each* dried

Hot sauce or red wine vinegar, optional

4 thick slices bacon or 8 thin slices baguette for garnish, optional

1 Preheat oven to 400° F. Cut the sweet potato, squash, turnip, potato, carrots and parsnips into 2-inch dice. Divide vegetables between two sheet pans and drizzle well with olive oil. Sprinkle with garlic, salt and pepper. Toss well. Place pans in oven and roast until vegetables are tender, but crisp at the edges, 30-40 minutes.

2 While vegetables roast, in a large stock pot, sauté onions and celery in butter until browned and soft. When vegetables are done, add them to the pot, along with chicken broth, parsley, and sprigs of fresh herbs (rosemary, thyme, and sage) tied into a bundle with 6 inches or so of kitchen string. Bring to a boil, reduce heat and simmer for 1 hour or until all the vegetables are tender.

3 If using bacon for garnish, fry 4 strips until crisp, drain on paper towels and crumble. If making croutons, brush 8 thin slices baguette with olive oil, sprinkle with salt and pepper and grill for 2 minutes on each side on a stovetop grill or toast in the oven for 10 minutes at 400° F.

4 When all ingredients in the pot are tender, puree soup using an immersion blender or in a food processor or blender in batches. Return soup to the pot, taste and adjust seasonings. Try a splash of red wine vinegar or a few drops of hot sauce to give the flavor a boost. Remove herb bundle. Serve soup hot, garnished with bacon or croutons.

Make it a Meal

Accompaniments:

A platter of cheese and fruit, such as Cheddar and apples, would round out this meal nicely. If using the bacon garnish, a grilled cheese-and-tomato sandwich would be perfect for a larger meal. For a lighter meal, serve Pear-Grilled Fig Salad with Goat Cheese, Walnuts, and Arugula* after the soup.

Wine:

Budget: Rich, dark Garnacha from Spain (aka Grenache). No bitter tannins needed. Special occasion: Chateauneuf-du-Pape. End of story. Any will do.

Dessert:

Individual Kiwi Tarts* or sautéed apples over frozen vanilla yogurt, if you didn't serve apples and cheese.

Lemon Split Pea Soup with Sour Cream

serves 6

Split Pea is the quintessential soup you hated as a kid and love as an adult. Most of us have to get past a certain age to overcome eating food that looks like it came out of a Gerber jar. There's a point, though, when it turns into supreme comfort food and when it does, try this version with a piquant dash of lemon, along with a small spoonful of sour cream. Since you're all grown up now, there's also lots of black pepper at the end, if you like. Crunchy seeded tortilla chips are nice for scooping.

2 tablespoons olive oil

3 stalks celery, chopped

1 onion, chopped

3 carrots, peeled and chopped

Kosher salt and fresh-ground black pepper

2 small red potatoes chopped (do not peel)

2 cups dried split peas

1 cup chopped ham

1/2 teaspoon *each* dried thyme, marjoram, and crushed red pepper

4 cups *each* vegetable and chicken stock

1 cup *each* water and white wine

4-6 drops hot sauce

2 tablespoons fresh lemon juice

1/4 cup sour cream or plain yogurt mixed with 1/4 teaspoon fresh-ground black pepper for garnish

1 In an 8-quart pot, heat oil over medium heat and add celery, onion, carrots, and potatoes. Sprinkle with just a bit of salt and pepper and cook, stirring, 5 minutes or so. Add dried peas, ham, dried herbs, stock, water, wine, hot sauce, and 1 teaspoon each kosher salt and pepper. Stir, increase heat to high, and bring to a boil. Reduce heat and simmer, cooking until peas and vegetables are tender, about an hour.

2 Stir in lemon juice. Taste and adjust seasonings. For a smoother soup, puree all or part of this soup in batches in either a food processor or blender or, if you have an immersion blender, right in the pot. For a chunkier soup, leave as is or mash briefly with a potato masher. Serve hot with tortilla chips and a dollop of the peppered sour cream for garnish.

Make it a Meal

Accompaniments:

Tortilla chips (I like the seeded ones.) or whole wheat crackers and a cheese plate. If hungry, serve with hot Cornbread Muffins*, butter and honey.

Wine:

Budget: South African or Chilean Sauvignon Blanc. Special occasion: Alyce's favorite wine in the world — Sancerre, which is a Sauvignon Blanc from the Sancerre sub-region of the Loire Valley.

Dessert:

Cranberry-Ginger Bread Pudding*

Cook's Notes:

If you prefer a thicker soup, use four potatoes instead of two.

Next Day Pot Roast
Supper Beef Vegetable Soup

serves 10-12

Having a way with leftovers is the mark of a creative cook. Planning ahead for the next day's meal saves time and money, but sometimes it's the only way certain dinners can be made. I often make beef stew after making pot roast, and it's the best, according to my family. Occasionally, though, I have a taste for something lighter or with more vegetables — or I've made chuck roast — and can get one more meal out of the extras. This soup, with a few changes or additions, also can become a quick minestrone. Freeze it for up to a month, and on the day you plan to serve it, run the container under hot water until the soup block pops out; turn the frozen block into the slow cooker set on low to thaw and warm all day. It will be piping hot by dinnertime.

2 tablespoons olive oil

2 large onions, diced

1 cup celery, diced

3 large carrots, peeled, and cut into 1- or 2-inch pieces

3 large cloves garlic, minced

2 bay leaves

Kosher salt and fresh-ground pepper

1/2 cup fresh parsley, chopped

8 cups (64 ounces) chicken broth

4 cups (32 ounces) beef broth

Leftover gravy, optional

28-ounce can chopped tomatoes

1 cup fresh, frozen or canned green beans

1 cup finely chopped cabbage

1 cup fresh root vegetables or winter squash (I use parsnips and butternut squash), diced

Leftover root vegetables from pot roast meal (cooked potatoes, carrots, onions, etc.)

2 cups leftover pot roast meat, cut into 1-inch pieces

1 cup small pasta such as tubetti or elbow macaroni

Hot sauce

1 In a 10-12-quart stock or soup pot, heat oil over medium heat and add onions, celery and carrots. Cook 8-10 minutes, stirring often; add garlic and bay leaf. Cook 1 minute and season with salt and pepper. Stir in remaining ingredients, except pasta and hot sauce. Bring to boil, then reduce heat.

2 Simmer until vegetables are nearly tender, adding water or extra broth to keep soup from becoming too thick. Add pasta and continue to simmer until pasta is tender. Season with a few drops of hot sauce, to taste, and more salt and pepper, if needed.

3 Serve hot or cool completely and ladle into large freezer containers. Freeze for up to one month.

Cook's Notes:

Potatoes or sweet potatoes can be used in place of the root vegetables. For a closer to minestrone version, add a drained can of white northern or cannellini beans and a tablespoon each of dried basil and oregano. A few minutes before serving, stir in one cup of chopped fresh spinach and/or a medium zucchini, diced. Pass a bowl of grated Parmesan cheese at the table.

Poached Egg:

For a quick, nutritious breakfast, pour one cup of soup into a ramekin and crack an egg into the center. Bake in a 350 degrees Fahrenheit oven about 30 minutes or until egg is done to your liking. Sprinkle with grated Parmesan.

Make it a Meal

Accompaniments:

Grilled Salt and Pepper Bread* or plain rolls or biscuits.

Wine:

Fattier cuts of meat: tannic red like Cabernet Sauvignon. Leaner: Merlot or Syrah. Budget: Malbec from Argentina. Special occasion: Washington Merlot — you'll look hard for this high-quality wine but it will be worth the search.

Dessert:

Cocoa with a Kick*

Turkey Wild Rice Vegetable Soup with Sherry

serves 12-14

If you stay in Minnesota for any length of time, you're sure to encounter the local foods Minnesotans swear by. They include maple syrup, walleye pike (superb when fried), any food on a stick (they're big on state fair delicacies), Juicy Lucys (cheeseburgers with the cheese inside), red-all-way-through Minnesota strawberries, and, last, and best: Chicken-Wild Rice Soup. My turkey version of this famous soup is one of those fine meals you cook and serve in the same pot, letting your guests slide back into the kitchen for a second or third bowl. What they like best is the little pitcher of sherry, for seasoning, on the table. I've left out the traditional cream in the soup, but if you prefer, simply stir in a cup at the end and warm briefly — no boiling.

1 tablespoon *each* butter and olive oil

Pinch crushed red pepper

2 onions, chopped

5 carrots, peeled and cut into 1-inch pieces

4 stalks celery, chopped

1 fennel bulb, trimmed, cored and chopped

1 cup fresh parsley, chopped

2 teaspoons dried thyme

Kosher salt and fresh-ground pepper

2 cloves garlic, minced

12 cups (96 ounces) chicken stock

1 cup white wine

6 cups water

2 turkey thighs, skin removed

2 teaspoons poultry seasoning

1 cup wild rice, rinsed several times and drained

Hot sauce

2 parsnips, peeled and cut into 1/4-inch slices

1/2 cup *each* fresh or frozen green peas and corn

1/3 cup dry sherry for garnish

1 cup roasted, chopped walnuts for garnish (optional)

1 Heat butter and olive oil with red pepper over medium heat in a 12-quart soup or stock pot for 1 minute. Add onions, 1 of the cut-up carrots, celery, fennel, parsley, thyme and 1/2 teaspoon kosher salt with 1/4 teaspoon freshly ground black pepper. Cook 5 minutes or until vegetables begin to soften. Add garlic and cook another minute or two, stirring.

2 Pour in stock, wine, and 2 cups water. Stir well and add turkey thighs, poultry seasoning, 1/2 teaspoon salt and 1/4 teaspoon pepper. Bring to a boil, reduce heat and simmer 1 - 1 1/2 hours or until turkey is tender.

3 Remove turkey to cutting board and let cool several minutes. While the turkey is cooling, add rice and 3-4 drops hot sauce, to taste, to the broth. Bring back to a slow boil. After turkey is cooled, shred using two forks, and return to pot. Cook about 20 minutes, then add parsnips along with the rest of the carrots. Continue to cook another 20 minutes, skimming off fat as needed. Stir in peas and corn.

4 Continue to cook until turkey, rice and all vegetables are tender, another 5-10 minutes. Continue to skim off fat. Add more water or broth if necessary. This should not be a thick stew, but rather a rich, brothy soup. Taste and adjust seasonings.

Special note:

Spaniards have a rating system in the region of Rioja, and it is based on how long the wine is aged.

Joven = less than a year of age.
Crianza = two years of age, at least six months in a barrel, then aged in the bottle before release.
Reserva = three years of age, at least twelve months in a barrel.
Gran Reserva = five years of age, at least eighteen months in a barrel.

Not all Crianzas are meant to grow up to be Gran Reservas, and Gran Reservas are not made every year. They are only made from the best vineyards and the best growing seasons.

Make it a Meal

Accompaniments:

Serve over or with biscuits. Pour sherry into a small pitcher and pass at the table with the walnuts, if using, to garnish soup.

Wine:

With its Italian roots, a Sangiovese based wine seems pretty obvious. Tempranillo would work just as easily. On a budget, let's try some Tempranillo, the national grape of Spain. It's the main grape in the wine Rioja, and easily located in any wine shop. Not overly tannic at the Crianza level, and very affordable. Special occasion, especially if you are adding meats to this soup, Reservas or Gran Reservas from Rioja would be super.

Dessert:

Cranberry-Ginger Bread Pudding*

Cook's Notes:

Be sure to purchase hand-harvested native wild rice.

Vegan Chili

serves 8

There are so many kinds of chili in the world, and I love just about all of them. This vegan chili, full of squash, onions, beans, and tomatoes changes a little bit each time I make it, depending on what vegetables are in season or on the counter. Come summer, it's full of zucchini or yellow squash, but in the fall it might also contain butternut or acorn squash that I've chopped and cooked ahead in the microwave. An optional addition of sautéed mushrooms at the very end lends a "meaty" touch. No matter what, since there's no meat, this meal is done fairly quickly — I serve it all in one bowl with a scoop of brown rice mixed with cilantro and black pepper along with a little spinach salad with lime vinaigrette. You might freeze leftovers in individual containers for lunches. Or make a double batch, freeze the second and skip cooking one night next month.

2 tablespoons olive oil

3 teaspoons chili powder

1/4 teaspoon fresh-ground black pepper

2 large onions, chopped

2 tablespoons jalapeño pepper, veins and seed removed, minced

5-6 stalks celery with leaves, trimmed, minced

4 cloves garlic, minced

1 *each* red and yellow bell peppers, coarsely chopped

2 *each* small zucchini and yellow squash, trimmed, and cut into 1-inch pieces

28-ounce can chopped tomatoes

1 cup *each* water and red wine (all water for alcohol-free chili)

1 teaspoon ground cumin

2 teaspoons *each* dried basil and oregano

Generous pinch of cinnamon

1/2 teaspoon kosher salt

2 teaspoons Dijon-style mustard

2 15-ounce cans pinto or black beans (or a combination), drained and rinsed

Hot sauce

1 tablespoon red or white wine vinegar

8 ounces button mushrooms, optional, cooked with 2 teaspoons olive oil in a separate skillet

6-8 green onions, trimmed and chopped finely (white and green parts), for garnish

1 In an 8 or 10-quart stock pot, heat olive oil and add chili powder and black pepper. Warm a minute or so until fragrant. Add onions, jalapeno, celery, garlic, bell peppers and zucchini; stir well. Cover and simmer 10 minutes, stirring once or twice, lowering heat if the vegetables begin to burn.

2 Pour in the tomatoes, wine and water. Stir in cumin, oregano, basil, cinnamon and salt. Add mustard and beans. Shake in 3-4 drops of hot sauce or to taste. Bring to a boil, reduce heat to a simmer.

3 Cook 15 minutes, stirring occasionally, adding water if the chili becomes too thick or sticks. Add vinegar. Stir and adjust seasonings. Add cooked mushrooms if using. Garnish with chopped green onions.

Cook's Notes:

Brown rice takes 45 minutes to cook, so if you're serving it with the chili, start the rice first.

Make it a Meal

Accompaniments:

If served in a large, shallow pasta bowl, you'll have room alongside the soup for the scoop of brown rice mixed with chopped fresh cilantro and a mini salad of spinach topped with a squeeze of lime, drizzle of olive oil and sprinkle of salt and pepper. Sprinkle chopped green onions over the entire meal. For this option, you'll need 3 cups cooked rice and 4-6 cups fresh spinach.

Wine:

Zinfandel or Shiraz, but a drier rather than a fruity version. Special occasion: Sonoma Zinfandel (drier style) or best Aussie Shiraz you can afford.

Dessert:

It's a good night for an ice cream sundae — maybe vanilla ice cream with a chocolate sauce to which you've added a little cinnamon and ground cayenne.

Turnip-Pear Soup with Crispy Prosciutto

serves 8

This lively cold-weather soup topped with quickly fried ribbons of prosciutto is refreshing and filling, but isn't so heavy that it doesn't make a lovely lunch or a light supper. Make a double batch; you'll be surprised at how attached you become to a soup you might never have heard of. Not too far from our house is a small wine bar/restaurant with a smart, food-loving chef. One Saturday in October, he had a parsnip-apple soup with cream on the menu, and I was just wild about it. I went home not wanting to recreate it, but to try something similar without the cream. Next day, turnips and pears were on the counter, a little prosciutto was in the fridge, and soon we were eating this for lunch. I like my version a bit better because it has some heat, which the French-trained chef might not have added.

- 2 tablespoon butter
- 2 *each* onion, carrot, celery, chopped
- Kosher salt and fresh-ground pepper
- 3 cloves garlic, minced
- 4 each turnips and ripe pears, peeled and chopped finely
- 1 cup fresh parsley, chopped (reserve some for garnish)
- 1/2 cup white wine
- 8 cups (64 ounces) chicken broth
- Dash sriracha or other hot sauce
- 1 tablespoon olive oil
- 4 thin slices prosciutto

Cook's Notes:

Sriracha is a Thai hot sauce made from chili peppers; these days it can be found in most grocery stores. You also can use Tabasco or another hot sauce, but it will change the flavor a bit since sriracha, although it contains vinegar, has a somewhat sweeter component.

1 Heat butter over medium heat in a large soup or stock pot. Add onion, carrot and celery. Sprinkle with 1 teaspoon salt and 1/2 teaspoon pepper. Cook, stirring, occasionally, until softened, about 5 minutes. Add garlic and cook 1 minute.

2 Add turnips, pears and parsley. Cook, stirring, 2 minutes.

3 Pour in wine and chicken broth and season with sriracha or Tabasco.

4 Bring to a boil; reduce heat to a simmer and cook until vegetables are tender. Puree in batches in a food processor or blender, or if you have an immersion blender, right in the pot. Taste and adjust seasonings.

5 While soup cooks, make the prosciutto for the garnish. Heat 1 tablespoon olive oil in a small skillet over medium heat and add 4 thin slices prosciutto cut into 1/4 inch ribbons. Let fry a minute or two, watching closely and turning, until browned and crisp. Remove to a paper towel-lined plate.

6 Serve soup hot and garnished with a few ribbons of prosciutto and reserved parsley.

Make it a Meal

Accompaniments:

Egg Salad,* Goat Cheese Spread with Dill and Red Onion*, along with some sliced baguette or Bread Machine Whole Wheat Rolls*. Very hungry? Garlic Bread Grilled Tomato Sandwiches.*

Wine:

A reasonably-priced Rosé with a bit of fruit would match the pear, and its dry style would complement the prosciutto nicely. The French chef would be very happy! Special occasion: A Brut Rosé from Champagne or anyplace else making good sparkling wines.

Dessert:

Coffee and individual pieces of dark chocolate.

Ribollita

serves 6-8

Ribollita (ree-bo-lee'-tah) is the happy, singing word Italians use for leftover minestrone soup "boiled up" (the literal meaning of ribollita) and served over toasted bread to stretch the meal for another day or to feed a few more hungry friends. Think French onion soup gone big time with lots of vegetables and herbs and perhaps some meat. I like making it from scratch and enjoying the "second-day" version right off the bat. While the ingredient list looks long, you don't need to include every item. No cabbage, but you have spinach, go for it. No cheese rind? Skip it. This soup is all about using what you have. I've also included instructions for making ribollita using minestrone from the deli or grocery store. This meal adapts easily for vegan or vegetarian guests and soon will be a favorite at your table. While you're cooking, try singing REE-BO-LEE'-TAH to your favorite tune, such as "America" from West Side Story. Don't forget to dance.

6 ciabatta rolls, cut in half or 12 slices baguette

4 tablespoons olive oil

1 large onion, chopped

3 stalks celery, chopped

5 cloves garlic, minced

3 large carrots, trimmed, peeled and diced

4 slices bacon, pancetta or ham, chopped

6-ounce can tomato paste

28-ounce can chopped tomatoes

8 cups (64 ounces) chicken broth

2 cups fresh spinach, chopped

1 cup cabbage, shredded

1 tablespoon *each* dried oregano and basil

1 bay leaf

1 teaspoon Herbes de Provence or crushed rosemary

Kosher salt and fresh-ground black pepper

Parmesan rind, 2-inchx1-inch piece

2 15-ounce cans white beans (cannellini or northern), drained and rinsed

1/2 cup fresh basil julienned (sliced very thinly) for garnish, optional

Hot sauce

1 Heat oven to 350° F. Brush sliced ciabatta with two tablespoons olive oil, place on a baking sheet, and toast for 5 minutes or so or until golden. Remove from the oven and set aside.

2 In 10-12-quart soup or stock-pot, heat two tablespoons olive oil over medium heat and add onion, celery, garlic, carrots and ham. Sauté, stirring often, until vegetables are tender. Add tomato paste, tomatoes, broth, spinach, cabbage, herbs, 1/2 teaspoon each kosher salt and fresh-ground pepper, and cheese rind. Bring to a boil, then lower heat to a simmer and stir often until spinach and cabbage are tender. Stir in beans. This soup should be thick, but if it's thicker than you like, add a cup of water or broth. Taste and adjust seasonings, adding a little hot sauce, if desired. (Put the hot sauce on the table for those who like a zippier soup.)

3 Place toasted bread in bowls and ladle soup over them. Use half of the cheese to sprinkle on top, along with the fresh basil. Pass the rest of the cheese and hot sauce at the table.

Make it a Meal

Accompaniments:

Since this soup is full of bread, you may not need much more to make a meal. If you have really hungry people, pass a plate of pepperoncinis and sliced salami or crunchy fresh vegetables like bell peppers, celery and cucumbers. My Lemoned Greens* without the goat-cheese toast, would be a simple, fresh side.

Wine:

Budget: Easily located Rioja Crianza (2-year old Spanish wine from the tempranillo grape). Special occasion: An older Rioja like a Rioja Reserva (3 years) or Gran Reserva (5 years).

Dessert:

Spumoni or lemon gelato

45

Cook's Notes:

If you'd like a meatier soup, add some more chopped ham or cooked, sliced Italian sausage, shredded cooked chicken or cooked meatballs. I often add a small, chopped zucchini during the last few minutes of cooking. Green beans or fresh peas are beautiful additions to this soup, as are many other fresh vegetables. For a vegetarian version, leave out all of the meat and use vegetable broth. A vegan version also omits the cheese.

Directions for making Ribollita with purchased Minestrone:

2-3 quarts prepared Minestrone soup from the deli or grocery store

Oregano, pepper, basil, garlic, rosemary, thyme, (optional, adjust to taste)

1 15-ounce can white beans (cannellini or northern), drained and rinsed

1 Preheat oven to 350° F. Carefully pour the minestrone into a 6-quart saucepan and heat on medium. Taste for seasonings. To make this soup your own, add a little oregano, some pepper, a pinch of basil, a tad of garlic or Provencal herbs like rosemary or thyme. You don't need to add salt; I can just about guarantee that one.

2 Stir in beans.

3 Follow the steps above for the ciabatta toasts and for serving.

Soups for Spring

Depending on where you live, spring can be warm, hot, cool, breezy, rainy, snowy or flat out cold. In Minnesota, we have coffee on the porch when it gets above freezing. While folks up north wait for the first bit of green in the lawn with bated breath, southerners have long since planted their broccoli and are eating fresh spinach.

These soups for spring cover all the bases. There's nothing worse than a spring cold, so my best and fastest chicken noodle soup, with all its inherent healing properties, is right here. There's a Saint Patrick's Day special of Potato-Corned Beef Soup with Irish Cheddar that's fun for a crowd; don't forget the Irish Soda Bread! When the peas come in — or you find some in your freezer — try your hand at clam chowder; you'll be surprised at how easy it is. And on that first day you can sneak brunch on the patio (Mother's Day?), invite everyone for Roasted Shrimp Bloody Mary Soup, along with an egg casserole, fruit salad and biscuits with butter.

I Have a Spring Cold Chicken Noodle Soup

serves 6-8

While it seems to improve cold symptoms, chicken noodle soup is America's favorite any time — even when we don't have the sniffles. This particular version features short prep and cooking time, inexpensive boneless, skinless chicken thighs, frozen egg noodles (both easily kept in your freezer) and an in-your-pantry list of fresh vegetables. You can make it for yourself if you're not too sick, but it's so much more comforting if someone makes it for you.

You won't believe how easily you can get to a pot of chicken soup! Fresh herbs make all the difference to this pot of goodness, though it's fine without them. If it's spring or summer, sow some herb seeds and grow your own. Frozen noodles are a worth-buying convenience. Otherwise, Kluski, or other dry noodles, are a good substitute. For easy prep, chop the vegetables the night before, or use the food processor, and you're nearly to dinner. Set the table, walk the dog, pour the wine and soup's on. Even my husband, who made this for me the last time I was sick, says it's the best thing he's ever made — he's not a soup maker.

1 tablespoon *each*: olive oil and butter

Pinch of crushed red pepper, optional

1 1/2 pounds boneless, skinless chicken thighs, cut into 1 1/2 -inch pieces

Kosher salt, fresh-ground black pepper

1 large onion, chopped

1 cup celery, chopped

3-4 carrots, peeled and cut into 1/2-inch pieces

2 garlic cloves, peeled and minced

1/2 cup fresh parsley, chopped

1 tablespoon fresh rosemary, minced (1 teaspoon dried)

2 tablespoons fresh tarragon or thyme minced (1 teaspoon dried)

8 cups (64 ounces) low-sodium chicken broth or make your own

1 cup water

2-3 drops hot sauce, or to taste

12 oz. frozen noodles, such as Reames

1/2 cup frozen peas

1 In a 6-8 quart soup pot or Dutch oven, heat olive oil and butter with the crushed red pepper over medium-high heat for a minute. Salt and pepper chicken thighs generously on both sides. Place them in the pan without crowding. Cook until well-browned, 4-5 minutes. Turn and brown the other side.

2 After you turn the thighs, add the onion, celery, carrots, garlic, parsley, rosemary and tarragon. Sprinkle with salt and pepper. Let cook, stirring occasionally, another 5-10 minutes until vegetables soften.

3 Pour in stock and water. Add hot sauce to taste. Bring to a boil. Reduce heat and simmer about 10 minutes.

4 Add frozen noodles. Return to boil. Reduce to a rolling boil and cook a bit less than package directions — 15 minutes or so. During last five minutes of cooking, stir in frozen peas.

5 Taste, adjust seasonings and serve hot. Store leftovers tightly covered in the refrigerator up to three days. I don't recommend freezing this soup because noodles don't freeze particularly well.

Cook's Notes:

Access your creative cook and use this soup method for chicken vegetable, chicken minestrone or "eat it once/eat it twice/eatin' chicken soup with rice" à la Maurice Sendak.

Make it a Meal

Accompaniments:

Green salad with fresh herbs and Alyce's Balsamic Vinaigrette*

Wine:

Since this is a comfort/cold-cure soup, my first choice would be "whatever the hell I want." And second, "whatever the hell I want to spend on it." I'd go with Chardonnay. It's so good, comes in so many types, very versatile. A little vanilla from oak would be good, Meursault from France would be tough to beat.

Dessert:

Strawberry Shortcake* or Blondies*

Cook's Notes:

I'm a firm believer in the healing powers of soup. This comforting Sick Day Soup comes from my mom, Fay McClendon. Pour 1 cup hot milk over buttered and sugared toast. (It also makes a tasty breakfast for a chilly morning.)

Alyce's Asparagus Soup

serves 6-8

My very first crush on a cookbook occurred when The Silver Palate Cookbook, by Sheila Lukins and Julee Rosso, was published in 1982. Before Silver Palate, the cookbooks I owned were more like encyclopedias, or sometimes worse, published by women's groups. My Betty Crocker, a wedding gift from one of my college professors, was perhaps the exception. With Silver Palate, my eyes and fingers ran from this to that in this new, incredible and beautifully illustrated book; I wanted to stay home from work and cook! An early favorite was Cream of Asparagus Soup on page 149. I served it cold as a first course for my daughter's baptismal party (along with Chicken Marabella—who knew the name it would soon have) and I'm pretty sure most of my guests hadn't eaten cold soup before. In a thermos, cold, this makes perfect picnic or traveling food with some cheese and bread. I have a small note on the page, "OK warm, too!"

Over the years, that asparagus soup changed and finally became this favorite version, which includes a spoonful of sour cream, as well as fresh tarragon and lemon rind for garnishes. Thank you Julee Rosso and Sheila Lukins! I know Sheila Lukins, who crossed the river way too young, is cooking in that perfect heavenly kitchen where the pancakes are made by Marion Cunningham, all of the Tupperware containers have matching lids, the ice never runs out, every lost recipe is found, all the olive oil is extra virgin, and the wine is always at the perfect temperature.

2 tablespoons butter or olive oil

1 1/2 medium onions, chopped coarsely

1 shallot, sliced

Kosher salt and fresh-ground black pepper

1 large garlic clove, minced

6 tablespoons fresh tarragon (or 2 teaspoons dry), divided

1/4 cup fresh parsley, chopped

2 pounds asparagus, trimmed and chopped

6-8 cups (42-48 ounces) chicken broth, unsalted

3 carrots

1 stalk celery with leaves

4-6 drops hot sauce

1/4 cup low-fat sour cream

Lemon rind

1 In a 6-quart stockpot, heat butter or oil over medium-low, and add chopped onions and shallots. Sauté about 10 minutes and then add garlic. Cook another 5 minute or until vegetables are very soft. Add 1/2 teaspoon salt, 1/4 teaspoon pepper, 4 tablespoons fresh tarragon, parsley and asparagus; let flavors marry by cooking 1-3 minutes, stirring.

2 Pour in 6 cups chicken stock; add carrot and celery. Add the hot sauce, to taste. Cover and bring to a boil. Lower heat and simmer 40 minutes or until all the vegetables are very tender. During cooking, add another cup or two of stock if it seems too thick. Taste and adjust seasonings.

3 Serve as is, or puree using an immersion blender or in batches in the food process or blender.

4 If you've pureed it, pour the soup back into the pan to rewarm or let cool and chill to serve cold. Top with a spoonful of sour cream, a sprinkle (not too much) of tarragon and a grate or two of fresh lemon rind.

Make it a Meal

Accompaniments:

Tapenade Salad with Hot Tomatoes and Goat Cheese Crostini * (see salad section) or Tuna-Cannellini Bean Salad*

Wine:

Usually a brutal pairing with wine, asparagus is so astringent and makes most wines turn bitter. I'd stay away from really fruity wines and steer more toward grassy ones to match the green notes of the asparagus. Which leads me to Sauvignon Blanc, but not from New Zealand. Not knocking NZ, it's just too grapefruity for this dish. On a budget: The best California SB you can afford or a young, crisp Italian white like Vermintino or Verdicchio. Special occasion: Sancerre, from the Loire Valley of France. These SBs have a mineral note I just love. Or, if you can find a killer Pinot Grigio from Alto Adige of Italy, that would be a little slice. Hard to find, but Austrian Gruner Veltliner could be a backup plan.

Dessert:

Strawberry Shortcake* or strawberries dipped in sour cream, then in brown sugar.

Curried Roasted Cauliflower Soup

serves 8

Although cauliflower is more of a late summer, early fall vegetable, I'll admit I enjoy it in the spring when a light soup appeals or for dinner after I've had a big lunch. The warmth of the curry can be increased, if you like. I use a fairly sweet curry powder; some are hotter. All-pears or all-apples would work just as well. If you stick to vegetable stock, this becomes a hearty vegan entrée with the addition of some thick whole-wheat bread spread with nut butter. For hungry carnivores, add a meaty sandwich.

2 heads cauliflower, cut into florets

2 apples, peeled, cut into eighths

2 large onion, peeled, cut into eighths

8 teaspoons olive oil, divided

Kosher salt and fresh-ground black pepper

2 shallots, cut in large pieces

3 garlic cloves, sliced

2 small carrot, peeled, minced

2 stalks celery, minced

2 ripe pears, peeled, cut up

2 teaspoons curry powder, divided

2/3 cup parsley, chopped

1/2 teaspoon each: cinnamon, crushed red pepper

8 cups (64 ounces) chicken or vegetable stock

1 cup *each*: white wine and water (or 2 cups water)

1/2 teaspoon kosher salt

1/4 teaspoon fresh-ground white pepper

Hot sauce, for garnish

Cook's Notes:

This soup doesn't have vibrant color. If that is something you'd like to change, add a big pinch of saffron along with the curry powder.

1 Preheat oven to 350° F. On a large, rimmed baking sheet, place cauliflower, onion and apple. Drizzle with 4 teaspoons of the olive oil, sprinkle generously with salt and pepper, and toss until well-combined. Place sheet in oven and roast for about 30 minutes or until vegetables are nearly tender.

2 While vegetables are roasting, in an 8-10-quart soup or stock pot, sauté shallots, garlic, carrots and celery in the remaining 4 teaspoons olive oil about 5 minutes over low heat, taking care to not burn the shallot and garlic. Add pears, 1 teaspoon of the curry powder, parsley, cinnamon and crushed red pepper. Stir and sauté another minute or so. Add stock, wine and/or water, salt and pepper and stir. Bring to a boil and lower heat to a bare simmer.

3 When cauliflower, apple and onion are roasted, add them to the stockpot and stir. Bring soup to a boil and lower heat to a slow boil. Add the rest of curry powder. Cook 5-10 minutes or until everything in the pot is very tender. Puree in batches carefully in a food processor or blender, or in the pot if you have an immersion blender. Taste, adjust seasonings, and serve hot. Pass hot sauce at the table.

Cook's Notes:

A quicker method is to roast all of the vegetables and fruit at once (except parsley), then add to stock, herbs, spices and puree. Omitting the fruit and other vegetables will give you a more pronounced cauliflower-flavored soup, as well as speed up prep.

Make it a Meal

Accompaniments:

Meatloaf Panini* and/or Tapenade Salad.* Or whole-wheat toast and any nut butter for a lighter meal.

Wine:

Let's see, garlic, apples, curry, cinnamon. You'll need something fairly complex here. My first option would be to drink whatever wine you used to make the soup. Big believer in "if it's not good enough to drink, it's not good enough to cook with." On a budget: Chenin Blanc. Makes a wide variety of styles, from sweet to dry. I'd stay away from the sweet (they tend to come from France), look for a nice balance of fruit and acidity. Special occasion: Savennieres from the Loire Valley. Yeah, I just said to stay away from France, but this won't be cheap. It will be dry. It will be special. You won't have any wine left. You'll wish you had another bottle.

Dessert:

Tin Roof Sundae* in honor of our cover artist, Daniel Craig, who can't pass up a Tin Roof for love nor money.

Tomato-Carrot Soup with Feta

Everyone loves Tomato-Basil Soup, often swooning with cream or Parmesan cheese. However, this is not *that* soup, despite the fact that there is basil in the soup and maybe a little cheese on the bread. Voted one of the favorite soups by testers, Tomato-Carrot Soup is light with a touch of sweetness and most happy with a big piece of toasted bread dunked right in the middle. Or it would kiss a companion grilled cheese sandwich because that's what tomato soup does, right?

This soup also makes a delicious first course for special or holiday meals and could take the place of a green salad. It can be kept warm easily in a crock-pot in the dining room while you prepare the rest of the meal. Then you'll hear, "Oh wow! You made soup!"

2 tablespoons butter

5 medium carrots, peeled, minced

6 stalks celery, minced

2 onions, minced

8 cloves garlic, minced

1/2 cup parsley, chopped finely

1/2 cup fresh basil, chopped finely

28-ounce can whole tomatoes (I like Cento)

6 cups (48 ounces) low-sodium chicken broth

3/4 teaspoon kosher salt

1/2 teaspoon fresh-ground black pepper

2/3 cup feta cheese, crumbled, for garnish

1 In an 8-quart stockpot, melt butter over medium heat and add carrots, celery and onions. Sauté five minutes, adding garlic during last two minutes. Stir in fresh herbs and tomatoes, breaking up tomatoes with a fork or knife. Let cook briefly, 1-2 minutes, then add broth, salt and pepper.

2 Bring to a boil. Immediately reduce to simmer until all of the vegetables are tender, 10-15 minutes. Add extra water or broth if soup becomes too thick. Taste and adjust seasonings. Serve hot.

3 Ladle into bowls and pass feta cheese at the table.

Make it a Meal

Accompaniments:

Salt and Pepper Bread with Parmesan Cheese* or grilled cheese sandwiches.

Wine:

With their higher acidity, tomato dishes need wines with some acidity in them as well, hence the popularity of Chianti with marinara sauces. If you're into a red with this dish, a Nebbiolo from Italy can be found fairly easily, and it's not too expensive, provided you stay away from the regions of Barbaresco and Barolo. If you're looking to load up on the feta, Sauvignon Blanc is a go-to match with that cheese. I'd stay away from an SB that's overly citrusy (here I go, bashing New Zealand again) and one that has more minerality to it.

Dessert:

Cheese Plate* and bread (if you haven't served grilled cheese)

Fresh Pea Clam Chowder

serves 6-8

Unless you live on a coast, you might not make clam chowder often; you probably lap it up in restaurants where it's a popular staple. One of my husband's very favorite soups ever, I came up with this simple and quick version using easily available and inexpensive canned clams, as well as fresh Minnesota spring peas to brighten up this white soup. You can leave out the half – and-half and use all milk, if you'd like. Don't forget the fun tiny round saltines called oyster crackers; the crunchy texture is a must!

8 pieces bacon

2 large onions, diced

4 stalks celery, diced

2 carrots, diced

1 teaspoon *each*: sea salt and fresh-ground white pepper (or black)

2 cups chopped fingerling or new potatoes

2 8-ounce bottles clam juice

Water

1/2 cup fresh or frozen peas

2-3 drops hot sauce

4 cups milk

1 1/2 cups half-and-half

4 6.5-ounce cans clams, drained

2 tablespoons butter

1/2 cup chopped parsley

1 In an 8- quart pot, cook bacon until well-browned, remove and drain on paper towels. Chop the bacon and set aside. Sauté onion, celery and carrot in the bacon fat until softened, about 5 minutes. Season well with salt and pepper. Add chopped potatoes and clam juice. Pour in enough water to cover all the vegetables and bring to a boil. Reduce heat and simmer until potatoes are tender, 10-15 minutes.

2 Add peas during the last couple of minutes. Season with hot sauce. Add milk and half-and-half. Stir in drained clams and butter and heat through.

3 Add fresh parsley and stir in bacon. Taste and adjust seasonings. Serve hot with oyster crackers; put the bottle of hot sauce on the table.

Cook's Notes:

If you'd like a thicker chowder, add another half-cup of potatoes.

Make it a Meal

Accompaniments:

Oyster crackers, Blueberry Muffins,* Toasted Almond- Broccolini Salad*

Wine:

The obvious choice will be Chardonnay, since you can easily find rich versions to match this rich soup. If you'd like to be a bit different, Viognier would work, as well. Usually a fuller-bodied wine and the aromatics are beautiful. Decent versions of both wines can be found at the inexpensive level, although it may be a little harder to find really exceptional Viognier. It will be worth the search, however.

Dessert:

Cocoa with a Kick*, blueberry cobbler (if you didn't make blueberry muffins) with vanilla ice cream, lemon cream pie.

Roasted Shrimp Bloody Mary Soup

While not exactly a cocktail in a bowl, this fun, festive soup does contain the vodka and celery for which Bloody Marys are famous. Blended and topped with a skewer of spicy shrimp, it's perfect for brunch when paired with an omelet and fresh fruit — and it's extra easy to throw together in the morning before guests arrive. It also makes a light first course for a grilled meal and could be served cold in on-the-rocks glasses. For fun, pass horseradish, Worcestershire sauce and celery sticks at the table. For a light lunch or supper, leave the soup chunky, serve over rice and place the shrimp in the bowl with a garnish of grated Cheddar cheese.

1   tablespoon butter

2   tablespoons olive oil, divided

1/4   teaspoon fresh-ground black pepper

2   onions, chopped

2   celery stalks, chopped

2   carrots, thinly sliced

1/2   teaspoon salt

1   bay leaf

1/2   cup chopped fresh basil, divided

2   cloves garlic, minced

1/2   cup vodka (or water)

4   cups water

4   cups (32 ounces) chicken stock

28-ounce can chopped tomatoes

24-ounce bottle Bloody Mary mix

1   pound shrimp, shelled, deveined

Half-sharp paprika or plain paprika with a pinch of ground cayenne

8   small wooden skewers

Grated horseradish, Worcestershire sauce, hot sauce, celery stalks for garnish at table, if desired

Cook's Notes:

I don't include any "heat" such as crushed red pepper, hot sauce, etc. since most Bloody Mary mixes are already spicy. If yours isn't, add a little at a time to raise the heat level to your taste. Hot Sauce can be passed at the table as well.

Preheat oven to 400° F.

1 Melt butter with one tablespoon of the olive oil and black pepper in an 8-10-quart stockpot over medium heat. Add onions, celery, carrots, salt, bay leaf and basil. Let cook 5-7 minutes or until vegetables are softened. Add garlic; cook one minute.

2 Add vodka. Bring to a boil, then reduce heat and simmer 5 minutes, stirring regularly.

3 Add water, stock, tomatoes and Bloody Mary mix. Bring to a boil, then reduce heat and simmer 20 minutes, stirring occasionally, or until vegetables are tender. Add more water if soup becomes too thick or is sticking to the bottom of the pot. Taste and adjust seasonings. Purée using an immersion blender or in batches in the food processor, unless leaving chunky.

4 While soup cooks, roast shrimp: Place shrimp on a rimmed baking sheet and sprinkle generously with salt, pepper, remainder of basil and paprika. Toss well. Roast for about 8 minutes or until just opaque. Let cool briefly. Thread two or three shrimp, depending on size, on each skewer.

5 Serve soup hot or cold in bowls or tall cups, standing shrimp skewers in bowls or cups. At the table, pass horseradish, Worcestershire, celery stalks and hot sauce.

Make it a Meal

Accompaniments:

Cilantro Coleslaw That Keeps,* omelets or frittatas, egg casseroles, rice (if serving soup unblended), grilled chops or chicken. Bread: Corn bread*, salt-and-pepper baguette, grilled flatbread or muffins

Wine:

You could just skip the wine and have a Bloody Mary. But I think a spicy Zinfandel would be just dandy, matching spice and spice. The trick with Zinfandels is that so many are just laden with all fruit, and you don't get the spice. So stay away from most Zinfandels from Lodi and stick with Sonoma. On a budget: Sonoma County Zinfandel. Special occasion: Single vineyard Zins from either Sonoma or Napa. If you find a Primitivo from Italy, it's the same grape, but will have a bit more acidity than anything from California. Harder to find, but I think it matches even better with all the tomato.

Dessert:

Fresh fruit salad if serving at brunch, otherwise Virgin Blond(i)es*

Corned Beef and Potato Soup with Irish Cheddar

serves 6

Perfect for that special day in March or for any other when you're in the mood for a potato soup unlike any other. Filling without being overwhelming and leaving room for lots of Guinness, this soup is finished off with a decadent cup of half-and-half and a grace note of grated Irish Cheddar.

2 tablespoons butter

1 onion, chopped

1 garlic clove, chopped

2 stalks celery, chopped

1/2 pound sliced deli corned beef, sliced into 1/4-inch pieces and cut in half

64 ounces (8 cups) chicken stock

4 potatoes, peeled, diced

1/4 teaspoon paprika

1/2 teaspoon kosher salt

1/2 teaspoon fresh-ground white pepper

2-3 drops hot sauce (or to taste)

1/2 cup chopped fresh parsley (reserve some for garnish)

1 teaspoon dried thyme

1 cup half-and-half or light cream

3 tablespoons cornstarch

1/2 cup grated Irish Cheddar, for garnish

1 In an 8-quart pot, heat butter over medium heat; add onions, garlic and celery. Stirring, let cook 1-2 minutes, then add the chopped corned beef. Cook for 3 more minutes until quite hot; add the chicken stock and bring to a boil.

2 Add potatoes and stir in paprika, salt, pepper, hot sauce, parsley and thyme. Lower heat and simmer until potatoes are tender, about 15 minutes.

3 In a small bowl, whisk together the half-and- half with the cornstarch. Whisk into the soup and let simmer until slightly thickened.

4 Taste and adjust seasonings. Serve hot and pass the cheese at the table for garnish.

Make it a Meal

Accompaniments:

Irish Soda Bread* and a platter of fresh vegetables and dip.

Drinks:

Guinness Stout or Irish whiskey, neat

Dessert:

Fresh fruit salad

Cook's Notes:

This soup isn't thick and heavy. If you'd like to make it thicker, increase the number of potatoes to 5 or 6.

Soups for Summer

I know. Summer doesn't scream, "Soup!" Bear with me; soup is fabulous in the summer. The vegetables are never better, and most summer soups are done in a flash, whether or not they involve cooking or are simply blended. And while I include some cold soups — Spicy Cucumber-Feta Soup, a favorite of my testers and their families, or Zucchini Soup Two Ways — I also have created some lighter warm soups like Coconut-Chile Chicken Soup and Salmon Chowder that you whip up with leftover grilled salmon.

I hate to single out a favorite summer soup, but it might be the Spiked Gazpacho, which is enough for a meal on a night when it's too hot to even light the grill. It can be served almost as a cocktail before a summer picnic, and it's my idea of heaven warmed up the next morning with eggs poached in it for breakfast. (The tequila will mostly cook out, right?) Just add a mimosa and make it brunch.

Thai Chicken-Coconut Soup with Vegetables

4 generous
servings

If made with *galangal* — a rhizome similar to ginger — this soup is similar to the popular Tom Kha Gai many of you know and love from Thai restaurants. A rich soup often served in small portions to start a meal, this is a lighter version that includes vegetables and rice and can be used as a main course. Despite a bit of slicing, this soup comes together very quickly and is a hearty meal that will leave your mouth humming with appreciation.

For a more authentic version, use galangal and kaffir lime leaves, but if you aren't able to find them, I've given options for using ginger and lime juice. A scoop of jasmine rice is the typical accompaniment for this soup, so start the rice first. As a last resort, or in the interest of time, make a batch of white rice in the microwave. If you don't want too much "heat" in your soup, omit the garnish of Thai bird chiles.

If served as a first course, don't include the carrots, cabbage and onion, and use the richer regular coconut milk (or part coconut cream) in place of the light coconut milk. You should have enough for six small first-course servings.

4 cups unsalted chicken stock

2 carrots, peeled and sliced thinly

1 small red onion, peeled and sliced very thinly

1/2 cup shredded green cabbage

1 stalk lemongrass, trimmed and cut into 1-inch pieces or smashed

1 teaspoon shredded kaffir lime leaves or several whole leaves, torn, with stems and veins removed (or the juice of 1/2 lime)

2 teaspoons granulated sugar

2 tablespoons grated galangal (or ginger)

2 teaspoons sriracha hot chili sauce

3-4 boneless chicken breasts, cut into thin, vertical slices

1 15-ounce can low-fat coconut milk

2-3 fresh mushrooms, sliced

Juice of 1 lime

2-4 tablespoons Thai fish sauce

1/2 cup cilantro leaves

2 Thai bird chiles (or serrano chiles) sliced very thinly

2 cups cooked jasmine rice

1 In a 4-6 quart stockpot, heat chicken broth over high heat. Add carrots, onion, cabbage, lemongrass, kaffir lime leaves, sugar, galangal and sriracha. Let boil 2 minutes and turn heat down to just below a simmer.

2 Add chicken slices and cook 1-2 minutes until no pink remains.

3 Add coconut milk and mushrooms. Cook another 2-3 minutes. Add fish sauce and lime juice. Taste and adjust seasoning, if necessary, using any or all: sriracha, fish sauce, ginger or galangal, lime juice, sugar. Try the seasonings in order, just a little at a time and taste before adding more or something else. Remove from heat. If you have used slices of lemongrass, remove them. (Food processor-shredded lemongrass can remain in the soup.) Serve hot with cilantro and chiles for garnishes and rice at the side in a small bowl.

Cook's Notes:

Fresh or jarred kaffir lime leaves and galangal may be found in Asian or specialty markets and occasionally in farmers' markets. Some Thai cooking ingredients also may be ordered online, including kits from amazon.com. Jasmine rice, traditionally used in Thai cooking, is readily available in grocery stores, but does take *40 minutes to cook*. If you'd like a vegetarian version of this soup, skip the chicken, use extra cabbage and you'll have Tom Kha Ga Lam Pli. For an authentic version and tutorial of Tom Kha Gai, visit the beautiful blog shesimmers.com.

Make it a Meal

Accompaniments:

Jasmine rice

Wine:

On a budget, the best Gewurz or driest Riesling available in the right price range. Stay away from the sweet ones. Special occasion, best you can find of the same. Alsatian Pinot Blanc would be tremendous as well.

Other Drinks:

Jasmine tea, or light, sweet beer

Dessert:

Ginger cookies with hot jasmine tea.

Black-Eyed Pea Soup with Yellow Pepper Salsa

8 servings

This black-eyed pea soup came together one noon when I just wanted something real to eat — something warm and filling, but not fattening. Contrary to common opinion or the instructions on the package, black-eyed peas do not have to soak, nor do they take two hours to cook. This soup, with its bright splash of crunchy Yellow Pepper Salsa takes about an hour to cook and doesn't cost much to make, which is just right if you want to serve it on New Year's Day for luck and/or to fix that nasty hangover.

Salsa:

- 2/3 cup chopped yellow pepper
- 4 green onions, minced
- 2 small tomatoes, chopped
- 1/2 cup chopped parsley

Soup:

- 2 1/2 cups dried black-eyed peas (approximately 1/2 pound)
- 8 cups (64 ounces) low-sodium chicken stock, divided
- 2 cups water
- 2 large onions, chopped

- 2 cloves garlic, chopped
- 2 smoked pork chops, chopped or 1 cup chopped ham
- 2 teaspoons dried thyme or 1 bay leaf
- 1/2 teaspoon *each* salt and fresh-ground black pepper
- 1 jalapeno (no seeds or membranes), finely minced and/or several drops of hot sauce
- 1/4 cup rice, uncooked
- 1 *each*, carrot and celery stalk, chopped
- 1 cup chopped fresh spinach or kale, optional

1 In a medium bowl, mix together yellow pepper with the green onions, chopped tomatoes and parsley. Cover and refrigerate.

2 In a colander, rinse peas and pick through, tossing oddly colored or shaped peas and stones.

3 Add peas, 6 cups chicken stock, water, onions, garlic, pork, thyme or bay leaf, salt, pepper, jalapeño or hot sauce to an 8 or 10-quart stockpot and bring to a boil over high heat. Turn down a little, but leave at a slow, rolling boil for about 45 minutes until peas are beginning to be tender.

4 Add rice, carrots and the rest of the chicken stock. Add a little water, if needed, so all ingredients are able to boil and move freely in the liquids. Return to a slow boil and cook until all ingredients are tender.

5 Taste and adjust seasonings. Add chopped spinach or kale, if using, and let cook another minute. Ladle into bowls and top with a spoonful of the Yellow Pepper Salsa or another salsa, if you prefer.

Cook's Notes:

You could go another flavoring route with this soup and replace the thyme or bay leaf with a teaspoon or so of curry. Quick Option: Use canned, drained black-eyed peas, unsalted, if possible. Cook the other vegetables and spices in the broth and add the peas once the vegetables are tender.

Make it a Meal

Accompaniments:

Cornbread*

Wine:

Love the New Year's Day idea, so I'd riff off that and serve some bubbles. Nice sparkling wines go with everything, including anything spicy. Not Moscato, that's too sweet usually. On a budget, I'd go with a Cava from Spain. Not as dry as Champagne, and not as pricey, either. Special occasion, how about a really great Brut Rosé. It will hold up to the spice as well as the pork in the soup.

Dessert:

Cocoa with a Kick* if you need "the hair of the dog."

Broccoli Soup with Brie Toast

6-8 servings

This soup is warm and filling without being heavy. Made with puréed broccoli and other vegetables, it appears to be a cream soup, but contains no cream. Topped with a bit of brie on a sliced, toasted baguette, it's a perfect lunch for guests arriving midday. Don't like cheese? There's also an option for a spoonful of Greek yogurt mixed with black pepper as a surprise garnish in the middle of the soup.

2 garlic cloves (1 chopped, 1 left whole to flavor oil)

1 medium onion, chopped

3 stalks celery, chopped

2 carrots, chopped

5 cups (about 1 1/4 pounds) fresh broccoli, trimmed well, and finely chopped

1/2 cup chopped parsley

2 tablespoons olive oil

Crushed red pepper, fresh ground black pepper, and kosher salt, to taste

1 1/2 teaspoons Herbes de Provence or a mix of dried basil, thyme and rosemary

8 cups (64 ounces) chicken stock, divided

4-6 drops hot sauce, or to taste

Zest and juice of 1 lemon

1/2 cup (4 ounces) plain Greek yogurt mixed with 1/4 teaspoon fresh-ground black pepper, for garnish (optional)

6-8 ounces Brie, cut into 1-ounce slices

Baguette or bread, cut into 6-8 slices 1/3-inch thick by 2-inches wide

Cook's Notes:

To speed up the cooking time, use leftover cooked broccoli or steam frozen broccoli.

Preheat the oven to 350° F.

1 Coarsely chop the onion, celery, carrots, broccoli, 1 garlic clove and parsley by hand or in food processor fitted with a steel blade.

2 In an 8-quart pot over medium heat, sauté in the olive oil 1 pinch each of pepper and salt, along with the whole garlic clove and Herbes de Provence for one minute. Add the chopped vegetables, stir and cook, covered, 5-10 minutes or until they begin to soften.

3 Add the chicken stock, hot sauce, 1/2 teaspoon each kosher salt, fresh-ground pepper, lemon juice and zest. Bring to a boil. Reduce heat to a simmer, cover, and cook until all vegetables are tender, 15-20 minutes, stirring once or twice while cooking. Puree the soup, if desired, in batches using a food processor, blender or food mill or in the pot with an immersion blender. Taste and adjust seasonings.

4 While soup is cooking, place pieces of bread 1-inch apart on a baking sheet, topping each with a piece of Brie. Toast in the oven 2-3 minutes or until golden. (Skip this step if garnishing with Greek yogurt.)

5 Ladle soup into bowls and top with the cheese toast. Or, spoon 1 teaspoon or so peppered Greek yogurt into the center of each bowl and gently push down until soup covers yogurt. Serve hot, although this soup also is tasty cold as is, or with the peppered yogurt garnish.

Make it a Meal

Accompaniments:

"Egg" Salad*, which is a green salad topped with a poached egg and a silky balsamic vinaigrette. Midsummer, try a small plate of ripe tomatoes and cottage cheese with crackers for lunch. For hungrier guests, or at dinner, serve additional bread, cheese, and/or sliced, cold meats such as salami or chicken.

Wine:

Lots of options to go with that soft cheese, Chardonnay would be the easy way out, and I'm not taking it! You've got plenty of veggies here, which leads me to Old World wines, and I think Vouvray would be a great match, made from the grape Chenin Blanc. On a budget, the Loire Valley of France is a huge producer of inexpensive Vouvray. The trick is that they are made in a wide range of styles, from sweet to dry, with no requirement of the producer to announce the style on the label. Some producers are helpful with words like Demi-Sec or Sec, which translates to semi-sweet or sweet. Depending on your personal preference for dry or sweet, get what you like. Special occasion, a truly great Chenin Blanc can be found (or special ordered) with a little effort. And the great ones will have the ability to age well, so don't fret if you find one that's more than a year or two older than you expected. They can last easily for 10 years if stored correctly.

Dessert:

Halved and grilled figs topped with a tiny spoonful blue cheese, a drizzle of honey and sprig of fresh thyme. No time? Stir together fresh berries and yogurt.

Salmon Chowder

4 servings

This chowder uses grilled (or cooked) salmon and is a good reason to cook an extra piece so you'll have enough for this main-dish soup the next day. If you made asparagus with the fish, you're that much ahead since this dish also calls for cooked asparagus. Unlike typical milk-based or flour-thickened chowders, this version is stirred up in a light, silky, broth. With just a breath of heat, it's gently comforting and filling. A tiny bit of heavy cream added at the end creates just a hint of satisfying richness. If you don't care for tarragon, try another herb, such as finely minced rosemary.

6-8 ounces leftover grilled or baked salmon

6-8 spears asparagus, cooked

1 tablespoon olive oil

1 medium onion, chopped

4 celery stalks, chopped

2 large carrots, peeled and minced

4-6 small, new red potatoes, cut in half

1 cup chopped fresh parsley

1 clove garlic, minced

Kosher salt and fresh-ground black pepper, to taste

4 cups (32 ounces) low-sodium chicken or vegetable broth

2-3 drops hot sauce, to taste

2 tablespoons fresh tarragon or 1 teaspoon dry tarragon

1 cup dry white wine or water

1 cup chopped fresh spinach or kale

2 tablespoons heavy cream

1 Cut the salmon and asparagus into 1-inch pieces and return to the refrigerator while you make the rest of the soup. Preheat oven to 200° F and place 4 oven-safe bowls on a baking sheet in the oven to warm (optional).

2 In an 8-quart pot, over medium heat, sauté the onion, celery, carrots and potatoes in the oil until the vegetables begin to soften, about 10 minutes.

3 Add the fresh parsley and garlic. Season with salt and pepper. Sauté, stirring, 1-2 minutes, being careful not to burn the garlic.

4 Add the broth, hot sauce, tarragon and wine; stir well. Taste, adjusting salt, pepper or hot sauce, as desired.

5 Bring to a boil, then reduce heat to simmer, cooking until vegetables are tender, about 15 minutes, adding chopped spinach during last 2 minutes of cooking.

6 Stir in the reserved salmon and asparagus, cook until they're warmed through, about 2-3 minutes. Serve hot in warmed bowls with a spoonful of cream and a bit of chopped, fresh parsley for garnish.

Cook's Notes:

For those who don't eat fish with dairy, omit the cream garnish and serve non-dairy sour cream at the table.

Make it a Meal

Accompaniments:

Goat Cheese Spread with Dill and Red Onion* on crackers or toasted baguette

Wine:

Chowdah not with clams? Great idea! I've said many times that Pinot Noir is a perfect match for salmon, and I'm not changing that stance with this soup. Beaujolais would be a good option, as well. On a budget, get a Beaujolais Villages, a step up from regular Beaujolais, but only a dollar or two more. NOT Nouveau. Special occasion, the best Pinot you want to spend money on. As this is not an overly earthy soup, I'd stay away from most Burgundies, but Central Otago from New Zealand, a cool-climate California, or Oregon would be great.

Dessert:

Peaches cut in half, grilled and topped with a drizzle of maple syrup.

Spicy Cucumber Soup
with Feta

8 servings

When cucumbers are plentiful and cheap, and the weather is sultry, it's time to make cucumber-yogurt soup. Originally Lebanese (Kh'yaaf B'lubban) and very like the Indian Kheera Raita, Americans have made this creamy, cooling dish their own. Perfect to eat as a cold first course or for a light meal, it's ready in the time it takes to whir a few ingredients through the food processor.

This is also a great soup to personalize: Add a bit more hot sauce or a pinch of cumin? Top with avocado or smoked salmon? Garnish with chopped scallions or tomatoes? However you make it, you'll want to serve this soup again and again. My own version holds some heat (skip the sriracha, a Thai hot sauce, if you don't like heat) and includes some salty feta and chopped red bell pepper on top.

I first encountered some of the flavors from this soup in Melissa Clark's fabulous Greek Goddess Dip (New York Times, "A Good Appetite," Feb. 10, 2010), which uses some of the same ingredients in a perfect, herby dip for fresh vegetables. When I began to test cucumber soups for this book, I kept returning to the combination of herbs in Melissa's dip.

If you don't have a food processor, simply chop the vegetables as finely as possible, whisk together the yogurt and buttermilk, and combine the ingredients using a spoon or large spatula.

4 English cucumbers unpeeled, sliced in half, seeded (pull a big spoon down the center of each half to seed), and cut into 1-inch pieces

4 tablespoons chopped red onion

4 tablespoons chopped fresh dill

2 tablespoons *each* chopped fresh basil and mint

2 cloves garlic, minced

2 cups plain yogurt

2 cups low-fat buttermilk

2 teaspoon sriracha sauce or a few drops of other hot sauce

Juice of 2 lemons, about 4 tablespoons

1 teaspoon fresh-ground black pepper

1 1/2 teaspoons kosher salt

2 teaspoons honey

1 cup *each* feta cheese, crumbled, and red bell pepper, finely chopped, for garnish

Cook's Notes:

Regular American cucumbers from the grocery store often are waxed, so peel them before blending.

1 Combine all ingredients, except feta and red bell pepper, in a food processor and blend until smooth. Taste and adjust seasonings.

2 Chill for a few hours in the refrigerator if you have the time. Divide soup between the bowls and top each with a bit of feta cheese and red pepper.

Make it a Meal

Accompaniments:

This soup is lovely all on its own, but if you have a hungry group, add some smoked salmon and crackers to the table or a basket of pita or naan. If it's not too hot, bake a batch of your favorite biscuits early in the morning.

Wine:

Sauvignon Blanc is a great go-to wine with feta cheese, and Pinot Grigio would be good, as well. On a budget, you should be able to find several inexpensive options for both SB and PG. If you like a bit of grapefruit, try a Sauvignon Blanc, especially from New Zealand. I think a California SB would match up a bit better; it usually has some grassy, green notes that will match the cucumber. If you prefer melon, go with the PG. Special occasion, you'll be able to find several high-end SB as well, less so with the Pinot Grigio. They are out there, you may need to hunt a bit. The most widely available option is Santa Margherita, which created the market in the U.S., but it's not your best option.

Dessert:

I love the idea of some fresh fruit and a bit of cheese with this soup — nothing more.

Zucchini Soup Two Ways

8 servings

When the zucchini are overrunning the garden or quite cheap at the farmers' market, make a meal of them. Luscious hot, this soup may even be better cold — especially as a first course outdoors on a hot summer's night or as a healthy light lunch. Easily doubled, it also can be made vegan by using vegetable, rather than chicken, stock and plain soy yogurt instead of sour cream. The second version leaves out the dill or basil, but adds a touch of curry for a very different soup.

4 tablespoons butter or olive oil

3 large onions, chopped

4 carrots, peeled and finely chopped

4 stalks celery, finely chopped

4-5 medium zucchini, chopped

3 cloves garlic, minced

1 cup chopped fresh parsley

8 cups (64 ounces) low-sodium chicken stock

Kosher salt and fresh-ground pepper

Hot sauce

1/3 cup fresh chopped dill weed or basil (or 2 tablespoons dry), with a little extra for garnish

2/3 cup low-fat sour cream or plain Greek yogurt

Walnuts or pistachios, chopped, for a vegan garnish

1 In an 8-quart stockpot, melt butter and add onions, carrots and celery. Cook over medium heat until nearly tender. Add zucchini. Cook about 8 minutes or until zucchini is losing its crispness; add garlic and parsley. Cook another 2 minutes.

2 Pour in stock and simmer until zucchini is tender, about 5 minutes. Add all but a few sprigs of dill. Salt and pepper to taste; add hot sauce to taste.

3 Puree with an immersion blender or in batches in the food processor or blender. You also can keep the soup chunky. Serve in bowls or cups topped with a spoonful of sour cream and a sprig of dill for garnish.

Cook's Notes:

For the curry version, leave out the dill or basil; add 1 teaspoon curry powder. For the curry or vegan version, top each serving with a teaspoon of chopped walnuts or pistachios.

Make it a Meal

Accompaniments:

Tuna Salad Quesadillas* or Irish Soda Bread*

Wine:

You had me at "first course outdoors." Sounds like a Rosé (not White Zinfandel) or light red would be nice here. Pink does not necessarily mean sweet. On a budget, Cotes du Rhone Rosé will be the easiest to find, or Rosato from Italy or Spain. Special occasion, you can really drop some dough on Rosé if you want, especially those from France. Or if you just can't abide by Rosé, a light red such as a Pinot Noir. Note: these are recommendations for the first version. If you are going to use the curry recipe, I'd switch to a heartier red that has some spice, such as Syrah/Shiraz or Zinfandel.

Dessert:

Choose from: Things to Do with Ice Cream, Fruit and Store-Bought Cookies*

Spiked Gazpacho with Crab

Is it a meal or a drink? You be the judge. The year I spent dreaming up this soup brought lots of interesting things to my already overly fertile mind. Not all of them turned out to be tasty, and some just made less sense as time went on. Sometimes I had another recipe that was quite similar, or the soup was simply too expensive to make. Spiked Gazpacho, on the other hand, was an idea that came about the same time as Grilled Shrimp Bloody Mary Soup, but ended up waiting impatiently a whole long year for testing, because who wants to test gazpacho with winter tomatoes? When I finally made it, during the last writing and testing of the book, I wanted to jump up and down and shout. It turned out almost exactly as I envisioned it, and now I know what we'll be eating (and drinking?) every August until we die.

Can you eat this in a bowl? Of course. You eat pasta with vodka sauce out of a pasta bowl right? But could you eat — or drink —this out of some fine, heavy crystal, on-the-rocks glasses, complete with a piece of grilled salt-and-pepper baguette notched so it hung on the edge of the glass à la sidecar? That's what we did, scooping the soup up with the toasted bread. Have a few tortilla chips nearby for when you've finished your bread. Try it.

12 slices baguette brushed with olive oil and sprinkled with salt and pepper

6 medium-ripe tomatoes (about 2 pounds), cored and cut into 1/8s

1 red bell pepper, cored, seeded, membranes removed, cut into 1- to 2-inch pieces

1 yellow or green bell pepper, cored, seeded, membranes removed, cut into 1- to 2-inch pieces

1 cucumber peeled, seeded, cut into 1-inch pieces

3/4 cup coarsely chopped red onion

2 cloves garlic, minced

Juice of 1 lemon

Juice of 2 limes

2 tablespoons red wine vinegar

1 1/2 teaspoons kosher salt or to taste

3/4 teaspoon fresh-ground black pepper

2 teaspoons sriracha sauce or 4-5 drops hot sauce

4 tablespoons olive oil

1/4 cup plus 2 tablespoons (6 tablespoons) tequila

Honey (optional)

Tomato juice

1/2-pound (8 ounces) lump crabmeat, picked over for shells and cartilage, for garnish

1 Bring an indoor or outdoor grill to high heat; place baguette slices on the grill for 2 minutes or until crispy and browned. Turn and grill briefly on other side or until browned. Remove from grill to a plate. Slice each piece of bread once from an outer edge to the center and set aside. The slice allows you to hang the bread on the side of a glass. Skip this step if you're using bowls.

2 Place or pour all ingredients, except tomato juice and bread, into a food processor and blend, pulsing, until well-blended but not smooth. You may need to do this in batches, depending on the size of food processor you have. If needed, stir in enough tomato juice to make 2 quarts of soup. Taste and adjust seasonings; you may need to add a bit more lemon juice, a drizzle of honey if the soup is too acidic or more olive oil for a smoother soup.

3 Ladle soup into small bowls or glasses, top with a spoonful of crab meat. Hang bread slices on sides of glasses or if using bowls, put it on top of the soup as a crouton. Pass extra hot sauce at the table. Serve cold. This soup will keep tightly covered in the refrigerator for several days.

Cook's Notes:

Make this is in the summer when the tomatoes are ripe, juicy, plentiful and inexpensive. If you don't have a food processor, you can chop the vegetables finely by hand or with a blender. You can easily leave out the tequila for a non-alcoholic version — add a little extra tomato juice to replace it. For a vegan version, omit the crab. I sometimes make an unusual breakfast by poaching eggs in gazpacho — a great use for using the soup the morning after the picnic. Soup for breakfast; why not?

Make it a Meal

Accompaniments:

This soup is a drink or could be a whole meal, and it's a perfect first course for a special breakfast or brunch where you might next serve a big omelet and fresh fruit. That said, there's no reason you couldn't serve it before a grilled meal at lunch or supper, as well.

Wine:

With all that yummy tomato, think Italian red. Barbera, from the Piedmont region, comes to mind. It's not heavy, matches the liveliness of this dish. Would prefer Barbera d'Alba over Barbera d'Asti. Know it may sound like splitting hairs, but the wines of Alba have more structure and hold up better with food, where the wines of Asti are more fruit-driven, more like a porch-pounder. If you want to splurge, I'd go with Nebbiolo from the same region. Unique in it's structure as well as acidity, Barbaresco region rather than Barolo region. Barolo might be too aggressive in its tannins for this dish.

Dessert:

Lime or lemon sorbet.

Guacamole Soup

4 servings

One of my favorite "instant" soups — there's no cooking involved! To make it even more instant, replace the first five ingredients with your favorite pico de gallo. Perfect for summer supper, part of what makes this soup so fun are the garnishes that make the soup different every time you serve it: crushed tortilla chips, tiny cherry tomatoes, sliced green onions, slices limes, chopped cilantro, salsa, extra hot sauce or a splash of white wine. Then just add a basket of tortilla chips or cornbread muffins and big pitcher of Malbec Sangria or frosty margaritas.

1/2 jalapeno pepper, seeds and membranes removed*

1 cup fresh cilantro*

1 small onion, quartered*

1 clove garlic, chopped*

2 large tomatoes cored and chopped*

2 avocadoes, peeled and pitted

1/2 teaspoon *each* kosher salt and fresh-ground pepper

2 tablespoons fresh lemon juice

1/2 cup buttermilk

1 cup chicken broth

Hot sauce

*These are ingredients for fresh pico de gallo. If you like, replace with your favorite salsa.

1 In a food processor, or in batches in a blender, process the jalapeno pepper, cilantro, onion, garlic and tomatoes together until smooth.

2 While pulsing, add avocadoes, salt and pepper. Next, pulse in lemon juice, buttermilk, broth and hot sauce, to taste.

3 Serve immediately or chill several hours or overnight. Soup keeps up to two days, tightly covered in the refrigerator.

Cook's Notes:

SANGRIA: A light drink that goes from cocktails through dinner, sangria isn't just for summer. Try it in the fall when the apples come in or at Thanksgiving with fresh cranberries and cinnamon sticks. In a large pitcher, stir together: 3 cups Malbec or other big-bodied red wine; 1/3 cup *each* of port and simple syrup, at room temperature; 1/2 cup orange juice, optional; 2 cups blueberries (mix with strawberries or any other summer fruit, sliced); 6 sprigs fresh mint. Refrigerate for 8 hours or overnight. Serve over ice and top off with club soda.

Make it a Meal

Accompaniments:

Skewers of grilled shrimp or scallops, tortilla chips or corn muffins*.

Wine:

Guacamole is a rich and spicy mix of flavors and textures, so a crisp, but mid-bodied white wine like Sauvignon Blanc might fill the bill and set it off perfectly. Other options might include an Oregon Pinot Gris or even an off-dry Washington (or German) Riesling if the guac is really spicy. Special occasion: a gorgeous American southwest sparkling wine such as Gruet would be very happy with both the guacamole and the corn chips.

You *could* also make Sangria (see Cook's Notes).

Dessert:

Dulce de leche ice cream or mango sorbet.

Salads and Fast Sides

When I go out to lunch, I nearly always look for a soup-and-salad combination. I still feel like I've had something special, but didn't cave and get the burger and fries. If I splurge and have a glass of wine or share a crème brûlée, I feel like I still haven't done too badly. At home, too, something crunchy or piquant next to a bowl of soup makes the meal seem fuller, more complete. This chapter includes not only a collection of much-loved salads and go-to dressings (see the Vinaigrettes section) from our house, but also a list of very quick put-on-the-table sides — everything from carrots to crackers.

A few of these salads — like Pear-Grilled Fig or Winter Squash-Mushroom — also can be whole-meal salads for lunch or dinner. Choose a savory or sweet muffin from the Breads & Spreads chapter, add a glass of wine, maybe an Individual Chocolate Pudding Cake, and your table is complete.

Simple Sides for Soup
Quick Additions to Make or Buy

Baguette or any Crusty Bread:

Best the day it's purchased, but some varieties can be wrapped in foil and frozen for 2 weeks. Try it:

Plain or brushed with olive oil, sprinkled with salt and pepper and grilled

Brushed with butter, sprinkled with grated Parmesan or any cheese and broiled

Topped with roasted red peppers or sliced tomatoes and broiled

Spread with yogurt, topped with sliced apples and drizzled with honey

Topped with deli chicken salad, etc.

Garlic bread: cut baguette into 1-inch slices, brush with olive oil or butter in which you've cooked a little minced garlic, place on baking sheet and broil briefly until golden and crispy

Croutons : cut into 1/2-inch dice, drizzle with oil, salt and pepper, and bake 15 minutes at 350° Fahrenheit.

Quick Additions:

Whole wheat toast: buttered or spread with honey or peanut butter. Don't underestimate it.

Cottage cheese toast: spread with cottage cheese and sprinkle with crushed red pepper or black pepper

Cheese, cheese spreads, fish spreads

Chutney with crackers

Tabbouleh tacos: stuff pitas or tortillas with purchased tabblouleh

Grilled or any sandwiches, cheese, meat, vegetable

Grilled tomatoes

Marinated asparagus

Sliced bell peppers

Olives or tapenade

Mozzarella balls and cherry tomatoes

Prosciutto-, ham- or bacon-wrapped asparagus

Cucumbers in vinegar with sugar and black pepper or in sour cream

Summer squash coins

Pickles, sweet or sour

Cottage cheese and fruit

Peaches and blueberries

Green beans vinaigrette

Fresh vegetables and salsa

Strawberries and sour cream

Apples and peanut butter

Celery and goat cheese

Sliced melon with mint

Couscous with vegetables

Lentil salad

Bakery quiche

Cucumbers, feta, onions and tomatoes with olive oil and vinegar

Tomato juice

Grilled cheese

Leftover grilled salmon on crackers

Tuna salad

Ham or salami roll-ups

Any green salad

Grilled zucchini

Goldfish crackers

Oyster crackers

Seeded tortilla chips

Purchased cornbread

Purchased biscuits

Pita or any flatbread

Cheese straws

Bread sticks

Wheatberry salad

Dried dates or figs

Dried apricots and cheese

Warmed or spiced nuts

Tips for Green Salads

Use the freshest greens, herbs and vegetables available. Grow your own, if possible.

Make sure the greens are clean, but also very dry. Wash and place them in towels, wrap lightly and store in the refrigerator at least an hour or use a salad spinner. Wash pre-washed greens, too.

Use a variety of colors and textures for appearance and taste. Don't be afraid to use a combination of cooked and fresh vegetables or fruit. Leftover grilled vegetables, poultry, seafood, cheese or meat are perfect for salads.

Make your own vinaigrette or dressing with the best vinegar and extra virgin olive oil you can afford. Use as little as possible, and toss the salad well.

Have really good, sharpened knives and use one cutting board for vegetables only. Meat needs its own cutting board, as does fruit.

Season greens with kosher or sea salt, fresh-ground pepper and lemon juice before adding vinaigrette.

Make your own croutons. Make your own mayonnaise. Neither is tricky.

Be creative! Look in the fridge, on the counter and in the pantry and make a salad out of what you have on hand.

If you're drinking wine with salad, go light on the vinegar or use white wine or lemon juice instead in your vinaigrette. You also can choose to drink a wine with a small edge of sweetness to balance the vinegar, like a dry Riesling or a Chenin Blanc. Salads deserve their own wine.

Grilled Asparagus with Texas Dip

4 servings

This is one of my favorite starters or sides and is delicious with any spring or summertime grilled meal, especially one that begins with margaritas. Served with soup, it makes a nice change from salad. Make extra for kids; they like dipping the spears in the sauce. If you don't have an indoor grill pan for your stove or an outdoor gas grill, sauté the asparagus with the olive oil in a large skillet.

1   tablespoon olive oil

1   pound fresh asparagus, washed, trimmed

Kosher salt and fresh ground pepper

Dip:

1   cup (8 ounces) plain, non-fat Greek yogurt or ranch dressing

1/3 cup salsa

Pinch *each*: table salt and fresh ground pepper

1   clove garlic, grated or smashed well

Make the dip first:

In a small bowl, mix yogurt or ranch dressing, salsa, salt and pepper and garlic. Taste and adjust seasonings. Set aside.

Heat outdoor or stovetop grill to medium-high. Brush with olive oil and spread asparagus on grill in an even layer. Sprinkle with kosher salt and fresh ground pepper. Grill, turning once, for 8-10 minutes or until just tender.

Place the bowl of dip at the center of a serving platter and arrange grilled asparagus around the bowl. Serve hot, warm, at room temperature or cold.

Cook's Notes:

You can make this dish a day ahead, refrigerating the dip and the asparagus separately. Serve cold.

Pear-Grilled Fig Salad
with Goat Cheese, Walnuts, and Arugula

2-3
servings

When you bring this salad to table, "oohs" and "ahs" will be escaping from everyone's lips. Almost dessert-like in its appearance, it nevertheless fills the bill for a bowl of greens and fruit before or after a great bowl of soup. It's also lovely all on its own for a special lunch. Blue cheese could be substituted for the goat cheese, balsamic for the sherry vinegar, or olive oil for the walnut oil.

3 cups arugula

2 ripe Bosc pears, cored and sliced but not peeled

2 ounces crumbled goat or my 2-1-2-1 cheese (omit for vegan option)

1/4 cup chopped toasted walnuts

4 fresh figs cut in half and briefly grilled* or 4 dried figs, chopped

Juice of half an orange

1/2 teaspoon sherry vinegar

1 1/2 teaspoons walnut oil

Kosher salt and fresh-ground black pepper

1 Combine orange juice, vinegar and oil and set aside. To toast walnuts, put them in a small skillet over medium heat, shaking the skillet frequently until they begin to give off a "toasted" aroma.

2 Place arugula in a medium shallow bowl and top with pears and goat cheese. Scatter walnuts around the edges of the salad and arrange the figs at even intervals. Drizzle with the juice, vinegar and oil. Sprinkle evenly with a pinch each of salt and pepper. Let everyone admire your handiwork before tossing. Serve at room temperature

Cook's Notes:

You can make this salad ahead of time and refrigerate, but add the pears, which will brown, and the dressing just before serving.

*To grill fresh figs:

Lightly brush a grill, grill pan or small skillet with olive oil. Trim stems from figs and slice in half. Place figs cut-side down and grill over medium heat for a couple of minutes. Turn and grill the other side. How long you grill the figs will depend on how ripe they are. The riper, the less grilling. If very ripe, don't grill.

Toasted Almond-Broccolini Salad

6-8
servings

I'm fond of salads made with cooked vegetables, and this tender-crunchy broccolini salad is one of my favorites. The broccolini — a hybrid of broccoli and Chinese broccoli, kai-lan — cooks just a couple of minutes with the shallots, garlic and almonds. Then come big thick shards of Parmesan cheese, slowly fried until they're crispy cheese chips. Combined with fresh baby spinach, warm tomatoes and topped with a mustard-cider vinegar dressing, this is one of those, "I can't stop eating this" salads. Serve before Tuscan Chicken Stew or Fresh Pea Clam Chowder or after Roasted Vegetable Soup.

3/4 cup sliced almonds	1/2 cup Parmesan cheese shards (use a potato peeler)
2 bunches broccolini (12-14 stems), trimmed	1 cup cherry tomatoes
2 tablespoons olive oil	6-8 cups mixed greens
3 tablespoons minced shallots	2 tablespoons fresh lemon juice
2-3 cloves garlic, minced	Kosher salt and fresh-ground black pepper
Salt and pepper, to taste	Mustard-Cider Dressing*

1 In a small skillet, toast 1/4 cup of the almonds over low heat 4-6 minutes until beginning to brown. Set aside.

2 Sauté broccolini in oil on medium-high in a large skillet. When broccolini begins to barely brown, add 1/2 cup almonds, shallots, garlic and salt and pepper. Sauté 2 minutes.

3 Add shaved parmesan. Cook until almonds are toasted and cheese is crisping and browning. Add tomatoes and cook until softened and begin to wrinkle and crack.

4 Place greens on a large, oval platter, and sprinkle with lemon juice, salt and pepper. Toss well.

5 Arrange greens in an oval ring around the platter. Place broccolini mixture in the center, surrounded by tomatoes.

6 Drizzle with half of the dressing; and pass remaining dressing at the table. Garnish with reserved sliced, toasted almonds.

Tuna-Cannellini Bean Salad
with Feta

4-6
servings

My tuna-bean meal is great for lunch or dinner when you're starved, but have little time to cook and haven't defrosted any meat. Or when you need something quick for last-minute guests. This American version of a favorite Mediterranean salad takes advantage of a well-stocked pantry. Even if you don't care for anchovies, try them here; they add a dimension and balance unavailable from other ingredients. Perfect for a hot day, this tuna salad is delicious any time of the year. Great with asparagus or tomato soup, it also pairs well with fresh sliced tomatoes.

2 6-ounce cans tuna, drained and flaked with a fork

2 15-ounce cans cannellini beans, drained, rinsed

2 stalks celery, chopped finely

8 scallions, minced

4 hard-cooked eggs, chopped

2 carrots, peeled and minced

1 cup fresh spinach or parsley, finely chopped

4 anchovies, smashed or minced, optional

Juice of 1 lemon

2 tablespoons red wine vinegar

4 tablespoons extra virgin olive oil

Generous pinch *each* of kosher salt, fresh-ground black pepper, crushed red or Aleppo pepper

1/2 cup feta cheese, crumbled or chopped

1/4 cup Kalamata olives, chopped, optional

In a medium bowl, combine everything but the feta and olives. Adjust seasonings to taste. If salad is a bit dry, a bit more oil. To punch the flavor, add a splash more red wine vinegar. Spoon into bowls and garnish with feta and/or kalamata olives.

Cook's Notes:

To make a quick "boiled" egg, lightly grease a small, deep, microwave-safe bowl and crack an egg into it. Poke the yolk once and the white several times. Cover tightly with plastic wrap and microwave at full power for about 1 minute. Let sit a few seconds before carefully removing the plastic wrap from the hot bowl. Scoop the egg onto a cutting board, cool briefly and chop.

Egg Salad

4 servings

There are times when a bowl of vegetable soup or a green salad isn't quite enough. If you had a little chicken or ham, you'd be tossing it in. Or, poach some eggs, whisk together a beautiful fresh vinaigrette and enjoy this satisfying salad. Lovely with Broccoli Soup with Brie Toast or all by its not-at-all lonesome self.

8 cups fresh baby spinach leaves

4 small tomatoes, sliced

4 carrots, sliced

1/2 cup parsley, minced

1 English cucumber, sliced into thin half-moons

2 teaspoons fresh lemon juice

Kosher salt and fresh-ground black pepper

4 eggs, poached

Alyce's Balsamic Vinaigrette*

1 Divide greens and vegetables between four bowls. Drizzle with lemon juice and sprinkle with salt and pepper.

2 Top each salad with a well-drained poached egg and sprinkle lightly with salt and pepper. Drizzle lightly with vinaigrette.

Cook's Notes:

For an easy poached egg, add a splash of white vinegar and pinch of salt to 3 inches of nearly simmering water. Crack an egg into a cup and, very slowly — giving it a few seconds to begin to set — slide it into the water. Let the egg cook gently for about 3 minutes (no boiling or you'll have a shredded egg) or until the egg is done to your liking. Remove with a slotted spoon; gently tap spoon on a folded paper towel to remove excess water before adding the egg to the salad. This may take a few tries to master, but it's worth the practice!

Tapenade Salad with Hot Tomatoes and Goat-Cheese Crostini

A visually stunning salad with big, bright flavors, this dish could be a meal in itself, but will definitely round out the menu when you're serving a light or blended vegetable soup. If you have a platter big enough, you can pile the tapenade at the center, surround it with the crostini, then arrange the greens around them and top with hot, spicy tomatoes.

Salad:

12 cups greens of choice (I like Romaine)	6 tablespoons olive oil
Kosher salt and fresh-ground pepper	1 cup tapenade (recipe on next page or purchase)
Juice of 2 lemons	Crushed red pepper
	2 cups cherry tomatoes

1 Place salad greens in a large bowl or on a large platter. Drizzle with a little lemon juice and sprinkle with salt and pepper. Refrigerate while you cook the tomatoes and make the dressing.

2 In a small bowl, whisk together until well-combined 4 tablespoons olive oil, 4 tablespoons lemon juice and a pinch each kosher salt and fresh-ground pepper.

3 Heat 2 tablespoons olive oil with a pinch of crushed red pepper in a large skillet over medium-high heat, add tomatoes. Salt and pepper lightly. Stir and sauté for about 5 minutes or until tomatoes are hot and beginning to burst.

4 Remove greens from refrigerator. Place tapenade at center of salad. Spoon the hot tomatoes over the surrounding circle of greens. Drizzle with dressing and serve immediately with goat-cheese crostini.

Tapenade:

2 cups pitted Kalamata olives or a mixture of green and Kalamata olives

1 cup fresh parsley, chopped

1 teaspoon fresh rosemary, thyme or basil, minced, optional

2 anchovies

1 tablespoon capers, drained, chopped

1 large garlic clove, sliced

Crushed red pepper

2 tablespoons red wine vinegar (or substitute lemon juice and white wine vinegar)

6 tablespoons olive oil

Kosher salt and pepper, optional

Mince olives, parsley, rosemary, anchovies, capers and garlic. Stir together with crushed red pepper, red wine vinegar and olive oil. Mix well, taste, and season with salt and pepper, if needed. Or place all ingredients, except salt and pepper, in a food processor fitted with a steel blade. Process, pulsing, until a finely chopped paste forms. Taste and add salt and pepper, if needed. Makes 2 cups.

Crostini:

Baguette, cut into 12-16 1/4-inch thick slices

8-10-ounce log goat cheese

Place slices of baguette on a large, rimmed baking sheet, top with 1/4-inch-thick round of goat cheese. Broil 4 inches from heat until golden brown and crispy, 2-4 minutes.

Cilantro Coleslaw

Saint Paul, where I live, is full of neighborhood family bars with kitchens. Not far from our house is a tiny place aptly named The Nook. When we first came to town, I Googled "best burger in Saint Paul" for my husband and up came The Nook. Unfortunately, it had had a fire and was temporarily closed. Finally they reopened, and we took our turn in line for supper one night. The burgers *were* awesome — their Juicy Lucy is top-rated and well-approved by Guy Fieri, according to the posters — but I was just crazy about a cilantro coleslaw that I thought needed only a bit of crushed red pepper to make it the very best coleslaw ever. So here's my version of The Nook's coleslaw.

Serve as a starter for either the 3-Bean Bacon with Kale Soup or Roasted Shrimp Bloody Mary Soup. And in case you visit Saint Paul: Bowling is available downstairs at The Nook if you'd like to work off your supper, but Lynden's Ice Cream Shop, featuring top-flight homemade old-fashioned ice cream parlor specialties, is also right next door!

1/2 head green cabbage, outer leaves removed, cored, shredded coarsely into 1/4" slices

3 green onions, trimmed and minced

1 large carrot, grated

Small handful fresh cilantro, chopped

2 tablespoons fresh mint, chopped, optional

1 apple, cored and grated, optional

Kosher salt

1/4 teaspoon each crushed red pepper and freshly ground white or black pepper

2 pinches white sugar

2 tablespoons white vinegar

2-3 tablespoons mayonnaise, to taste

1 In a large bowl, place cabbage, onions, carrot, cilantro, mint and apple, and toss well. Sprinkle with salt, to taste, red and black pepper, and 1 pinch of sugar. Add 1 tablespoon vinegar and toss well. Set aside.

2 In a small bowl, stir together 1 tablespoon vinegar with the mayonnaise and 1 pinch of sugar. Pour over cabbage mixture and toss well. Taste and adjust seasonings. Serve at room temperature or cold. Store tightly covered in refrigerator up to 4 days.

Cook's Notes:

If you'd like to make a nonfat version of this salad, omit the mayo. It's tasty with just the vinegar and seasonings as a dressing.

Greens with Lemon Vinaigrette and Cheese Toast

4 large
or
8 small
servings

A little something when only a little something is needed, or when you're looking for a citrusy bite to go along with a lusty soup like Parmesan-Peanut Spicy Pumpkin, this salad has a sparkly lightness on the palate. You taste and wonder what makes it so good, while it appears so very simple. The secret is in the freshest greens, well-seasoned. The fun crunch of a little cheese toast (who doesn't love that?) on the side makes it all come together.

Goat-Cheese Toast:

Make this first!

1/2 baguette, cut into 8, 1/2-inch slices

Olive oil

8 tablespoons goat (or 8 small slices other) cheese, softened

Kosher salt and fresh-ground black pepper

1 Preheat broiler and place rack about 4 inches from heating element.

2 Place baguette pieces on a heavy baking sheet 1 to 2-inches apart, brush lightly with olive oil and top each with a tablespoon of cheese.

3 Sprinkle each toast lightly with salt and pepper.

4 Place pan on broiler rack and let broil, watching closely, for 2 minutes or until just crispy. Remove from oven and set aside to cool.

Salad:

8 cups fresh, washed greens

Kosher salt and fresh-ground pepper

2 tablespoons fresh herbs (any kind), chopped

Lemon Vinaigrette*

1/4 cup sliced Kalamata olives for garnish, optional

1 Place greens and herbs in a large bowl and toss well with a sprinkle of salt and pepper.

2 Drizzle about half the vinaigrette carefully over greens and toss again gently. Add more if needed/desired.

3 Divide dressed salad onto four or eight plates, and top each salad with olives, if desired, and one or two pieces of cheese toast.

Winter Squash-Mushroom Salad
with Sherry-Truffle Oil Vinaigrette

6 servings

This "meaty" and attractive vegetarian salad makes a wonderful meal all on its own with just a pretty glass of Oregon Pinot Noir on the side. But pair it with a light soup, and you have all you need for a light supper on a cool fall evening. You can easily use balsamic vinegar and olive oil if you don't have the sherry vinegar or truffle oil, although these ingredients make the dish quite unique. Truffle oil is available in many gourmet shops or fine grocery shops. Also, cooking the squash in the microwave, rather than the oven, will put this salad on the table sooner.

4 cups cooked winter squash (acorn, butternut, etc.), peeled and cut into 1-inch pieces

8 ounces button mushrooms, sliced

1 tablespoon butter

5 sage leaves, finely minced or julienned and sautéed in about 1 tablespoon butter (about 1 tablespoon) with 5 leaves of sage finely minced or julienned

1/4 cup chopped fresh parsley

Kosher salt and fresh-ground black pepper

1 cup *each* fresh spinach and arugula

12 large shards Parmesan cheese (use a potato peeler)

Sherry-Truffle Oil Vinaigrette*

4 tablespoons chopped mixed almonds and cashews, for garnish

2 tablespoons chopped dried cranberries or cherries, optional

1 Sauté mushrooms and sage in about 1 tablespoon butter until mushrooms begin to release their juice.

2 In a large bowl, mix squash, parsley and mushrooms mixture. Salt and pepper generously.

3 Use a potato peeler to make the Parmesan shards or peels; carefully stir into squash mixture.

4 Drizzle salad with enough vinaigrette to moisten lightly. Toss gently, but thoroughly, until all ingredients are coated.

5 Divide the salad between four salad plates and top each with a tablespoon of chopped nuts and 1/2 tablespoon of chopped cranberries, if desired. Serve immediately.

Cook's Notes:

To cook squash in the microwave, pour 2 tablespoons water into a 3-quart microwave-safe dish. Carefully cut acorn or butternut squash in half, scoop out seeds and strings. Add a peeled clove of garlic or peeled shallot to each squash half. Place squash in dish and cover tightly with plastic wrap or waxed paper. Microwave on high about five minutes, remove from oven with mitts and, with a small sharp knife, check for doneness. You want the squash just tender, not mushy. If it's not done, put it back in the microwave and cook another minute or two; check again until the knife is easily inserted. Mince the garlic or shallot and add to the salad.

If you don't have fresh sage, use 1/2 teaspoon dry sage and rub between your fingers.

Green Bean, Mushroom and Jasmine Rice Salad with Mustard-Tarragon Vinaigrette

6 servings

Another lovely vegetarian lunch or supper all on its own, this hearty green bean salad makes an elegant second course following a bowl of Cucumber-Feta Soup in the summer or pair it with Spicy Red Lentil Soup come fall. Make extra green beans one night so the salad will be even easier to assemble the next day. The convenient microwavable packages of haricots verts, if available, make easy work of the green beans, too. I like nutty, jasmine rice, but any rice you have will work just as well. For color, chopped red pepper can take the place of the tomatoes. For a heartier meal, this salad makes a beautiful bed for tuna filets or grilled chicken. A very forgiving dish, you can make it just a bit ahead, cover and have it ready on the table.

3 cups hot, cooked jasmine rice

1 pound thin green beans (haricots verts) or regular green beans

8 ounces button mushrooms, sliced

1 tablespoon olive oil

Fresh-ground black pepper, kosher salt and crushed red pepper, to taste

2 tablespoons plus 1 teaspoon fresh tarragon (or 3 1/2 teaspoons dried tarragon), minced and divided

2 green onions, minced

1/4 cup sliced, toasted almonds

1/2 lemon

6 cherry tomatoes for garnish

Mustard-Tarragon Vinaigrette*

1 Cover hot rice and set aside; it will stay warm about a half hour. In the meantime, cook the beans for approximately 5 minutes in boiling water or 3-4 minutes on full power in the microwave or follow directions on the microwavable package. Thicker beans may take another minute or 2. The beans should be just tender, not crunchy, but not mushy. Drain the beans and toss with a pinch each of kosher salt and fresh-ground pepper.

2 While the beans cook, pour 1 tablespoon olive oil into a medium skillet and heat over medium-high. Add the sliced mushrooms and cook 2 minutes. Stir to turn, season with pepper, and cook an additional two minutes or so until cooked thoroughly. Sprinkle with a pinch of salt.

3 In a large bowl, add the warm rice, sprinkle with a generous pinch of salt, pepper and crushed red pepper and add the green beans and mushrooms. Toss well. Stir in tarragon. Drizzle with Mustard-Tarragon Vinaigrette; mix gently, but thoroughly. If the dish seems dry, drizzle with a bit more olive oil and toss again. Taste and re-season if needed. Spoon onto a serving platter. Squeeze the half lemon over the salad and sprinkle with green onions and almonds. Arrange cherry tomatoes on top. Serve warm or at room temperature.

Cook's Notes:

When using larger, thicker green beans, cut the beans into 2- or 3-inch pieces before cooking to make the salad more attractive and easier to toss.

Vinaigrettes

Alyce's (And Your) Balsamic Vinaigrette:

One fall, I obsessively made batch after batch of balsamic vinaigrette trying to get something I didn't just like, but adored. I came up with this version, but feel free to change it up a bit and call it your own. Do buy the best balsamic vinegar you can find; it makes all the difference and you'll thank yourself forever.

Makes 1 Cup

1/3 cup fine quality balsamic vinegar (I like Masserie di Sant'eramo.)

2 heaping tablespoons Dijon-style mustard

1 tablespoon honey

1 shallot, minced

2 garlic cloves, minced

Kosher salt, to taste

1/2 teaspoon fresh-ground black pepper

Hot sauce, 1-2 drops or to taste

2/3 cup good quality extra-virgin olive oil (I like Olio Santo or Ravida.)

1 In a food processor, combine all ingredients *except olive oil*, and pulse until thoroughly pureed and very-well mixed, or whisk together very well in a large bowl.

2 With machine running, slowly pour the olive oil into the tube on top of the processor and leave running until thoroughly emulsified. If whisking by hand, drizzle a tablespoon or two of oil in at a time and whisk until that olive oil is well incorporated before adding more. Taste and adjust seasonings. Keeps in fridge several days. Without the shallot and garlic, it will keep for weeks.

Lemon Vinaigrette:

2 tablespoons lemon juice

Generous pinch of salt and several grinds of white pepper

1/4 teaspoon Dijon-style mustard

4 tablespoons extra virgin olive oil

Slowly drizzle the olive oil, a tablespoon at a time, into the juice mixture, whisking steadily until well combined or emulsified.

Mustard-Tarragon Vinaigrette:

2 tablespoons white wine vinegar

1 heaping teaspoon Dijon-style mustard

1 teaspoon fresh tarragon, chopped (1/2 teaspoon dried)

2 cloves garlic, minced

Hot sauce, 1-2 drops or to taste

Kosher salt and fresh-ground black pepper

4 tablespoons extra virgin olive oil

Whisk together the vinegar, mustard, tarragon, garlic, hot sauce and a pinch each of kosher salt and pepper. Drizzle in the olive oil 1 tablespoon at a time, whisking all the while until the oil is incorporated, and the vinaigrette is thickened.

Sherry-Truffle Oil Vinaigrette:

I based this vinaigrette on one of Andrea Immer Robinson's from her excellent and invaluable book, Everyday Dining with Wine.

2 tablespoons sherry vinegar

1 1/2 tablespoons balsamic vinegar

1 shallot, peeled and minced

1 pinch each kosher salt, fresh-ground black pepper, crushed red pepper

1/2 teaspoon Dijon-style mustard

1 tablespoon truffle oil

3 tablespoons extra-virgin olive oil

In a small bowl, whisk together vinegars, shallot, seasonings and mustard. Drizzle in oils, whisking, until well-combined.

Mustard-Cider Vinaigrette:

1 tablespoon Dijon-style mustard

3 tablespoons apple cider vinegar

1 tablespoon honey

1/2 cup extra virgin olive oil

Kosher salt and fresh-ground black pepper

In a medium bowl or measuring cup, whisk together all but oil. Drizzle oil in slowly, whisking as you go, until all the oil is well incorporated, and the vinaigrette is emulsified. Taste using a piece of greens dipped into the dressing. Adjust seasoning as needed.

Breads and Spreads

Where there's soup, there's bread — or crackers. They fill us up, provide a spot for butter, meat or cheese, but most of all, let us indulge in the most fun aspects of soup eating: dunking or scooping. What is beef stew without a big hunk of crusty bread to mop the bottom of the bowl? Tomato soup without saltines? Chili without cornbread? And what would clam chowder be with no oyster crackers?

While any bread could accompany soup, this chapter presents a few tried and true gems to pair with soups in the book. Some are helpful pushers or something good to crunch; others, like the full sandwiches, make a light soup into a full meal. Cheese and fish spreads, including a homemade cheese, give you some tasty options for bread and cracker toppings.

Keep your pantry or freezer full of things you like to eat with soup. Pick up favorite muffin or cornbread mixes for the pantry or make extra home-made muffin and freeze them wrapped well in foil and stored in freezer containers. Have purchased crackers, wraps, tortillas or flatbreads on hand for instant sides.

Make friends with your bread machine. And if you don't have one, think about buying a good bread machine with a cookbook. It will make your life easier if you can start both the bread machine and a pot (or slow cooker) of soup at the same time. You'll love walking in the door to fresh bread and soup after work.

Take the time to discover where the best baguettes or crusty rolls can be bought in your neighborhood, since these breads are often a soup's very best friends. Cut hard rolls or baguettes in half, wrap in foil and freeze for up to two weeks. Then bake at 350° for about 15 minutes until they're hot and crispy and ready to dunk into your soup. Don't forget the butter — a little bit never hurt anyone.

Great-with-Any Soup
Bread Ideas

Salt-and-Pepper Bread:

Slice a baguette into 1-inch pieces. Brush lightly with olive oil; sprinkle with salt and pepper. Grill on an outdoor or indoor grill for 2 minutes on high or until golden brown; turn and grill the other side until golden. Serve hot or at room temperature.

Cheese Bread:

Preheat broiler. Slice a baguette into 1-inch rounds. Place on a baking sheet. Sprinkle each piece with some grated Parmesan or Cheddar cheese. Broil bread 4 inches from heat, watching closely, until cheese is melted, bubbly and brown. Serve hot or at room temperature.

Croutons:

Good use for stale bread and a great crunch for your soup. Cut bread into 1-inch slices, then cut in half horizontally and into thirds vertically so you have 6 pieces (approximate squares or rectangles.) Heat 1/4 cup olive oil in a skillet over medium heat and place bread in skillet. Cook until bread is crispy brown on one side, turn and cook on the other side, watching carefully to avoid burning. Remove to paper towel-lined plate and season as desired (salt, pepper, herbs, minced garlic) while hot.

Toppings or Stir-ins Make the Soup!

Finely chopped nuts

Grated or chopped cheese

Toasted bread crumbs

Crushed crackers

Minced onion, bell or hot peppers,
   tomatoes or cucumbers

Chopped zucchini or
   summer squash

Polenta, creamy or cubed

Cooked rice

Grated horseradish

Grated garlic

Whole or chopped fresh or
   dried herbs

Ground spices, such as paprika and
   various peppers

Drizzle of cream, sour cream,
   yogurt or crème fraiche

Spoonful of another soup

Pesto or pistou

Puree of tomatoes

Hot sauce or sriracha

Olive oil or melted butter

Vinegar or lemon juice

Cornbread-Cheese Muffins with Onions or Green Chiles

makes 12

Some people like their cornbread muffins quite sweet and tender, which is how they're often served in restaurants. Others prefer them on the savory side with onions or green chiles and a bit of crunch from the cornmeal. My muffins bridge the gap — just a little sugar and equal amounts of cornmeal and white, unbleached flour, with a hint of onion and cheddar cheese. If you like a crunchier muffin, increase the cornmeal to 1 1/4 cups and decrease the white flour to 3/4 cup. Sweeter? Use 6 tablespoons of granulated sugar and leave out the black pepper and onion. Less saturated fat? Use canola oil instead of butter. Although I call for either onions OR chiles, try your muffins with both. Experiment a bit to see how to make them just how *you* like them. Whatever you do, don't over bake your muffins, or they'll be dry and tasteless. This recipe cuts in half easily to make 6.

Softened butter for greasing muffin tins

1 cup each yellow (or white) cornmeal and white, unbleached flour

4 tablespoons granulated sugar

2 teaspoon baking powder

1/2 teaspoon salt

1/4 teaspoon fresh-ground black pepper

4 tablespoons butter, melted

1 cup milk

2 eggs, beaten

1/2 cup grated cheddar cheese

2 teaspoons finely minced onion, green onion and/or 2 tablespoons chopped, canned green chiles

1 Preheat oven to 425° F. Grease muffin tin well with softened butter. Place the tin in the oven to heat for 2-3 minutes. (Don't use paper liners.)

2 Mix flour, cornmeal, sugar, baking powder and salt in a medium bowl. In a mixing cup or small bowl, whisk together butter, milk, eggs, cheese and onions and/or chiles. Pour milk mixture into flour mixture, and stir until just well blended. Don't over mix.

3 Remove muffin tin from oven and place on pot holders on a flat surface. Pour or spoon batter, dividing evenly, into the muffin cups. Bake for about 15 minutes or until muffins are just barely firm, golden and a toothpick inserted in the middle comes out clean or almost clean. Do not over bake. Serve hot with butter. If you haven't made the green-chile variety, put the honey jar on the table, as well. Wrap leftovers well and store at room temperature up to 2 days or freeze up to 8 weeks.

Cook's Notes:

Use this recipe to make cornbread in a 9-inch cast-iron frying pan. Preheat oven to 400° F. Drop the softened butter into the pan and heat on the stove for 2 minutes, brushing the butter around to coat the pan. Pour in batter, let cook a 1-2 minutes, then bake in the oven 20 minutes or until golden and a toothpick inserted in the middle comes out clean or nearly clean. If using a regular 9-inch baking pan, place the butter in the pan and heat 1-2 minutes in the oven.

Blueberry Muffins

makes 12

Years ago, I worked for The National Trust for Historic Preservation. I held a variety of positions, but one of my favorites was running the bookstore and gift shop at Woodlawn Plantation in Mount Vernon, Va. Somewhere at Woodlawn, I ran across a recipe for blueberry muffins I made and adored. I changed and substituted ingredients over the years until I had this orange-scented beauty complete with just a tad of crunchy mouth feel. These are not the heavy, large, calorie- and sugar-laden muffins offered nowadays in many restaurants and bakeries, but rather small, light gems that melt in the mouth and shout for a second. They're great for breakfast, snacks or for lunch with a chicken salad, but I particularly like them with soup. Comfort food par excellence, tuck them into a tote when you travel by plane or car so you can carry home along with you.

Softened butter for greasing
    the muffin tin

2 cups unbleached
    all-purpose flour

1/4 cup stoneground cornmeal

1/2 cup white granulated
    sugar

1/2 teaspoon salt

1 1/2 teaspoons baking powder

1/2 teaspoon baking soda

1 tablespoon grated
    orange rind

1/4 cup melted butter

1/2 cup milk

1/2 cup orange juice

2 eggs

1 cup blueberries

1 Preheat oven to 400 degrees Fahrenheit and place oven rack in the center of the oven. Grease a 12- cup muffin tin very well with softened butter and set aside.

2 In a medium bowl, mix together the dry ingredients (flour through orange rind) and set aside. In another bowl, beat together the wet ingredients (butter – eggs). Pour the wet ingredients into the dry ingredients and mix until just barely combined. Do not over mix. Gently stir in the blueberries.

3 Using a greased ice cream scoop or large spoon, divide the batter among twelve greased muffin cups. Bake for 14-16 minutes or until the muffins are set, firm, and light golden in color. A toothpick inserted at the center should come out clean. Bang the bottom of the pan firmly on the counter to loosen the muffins and turn the pan upside down onto a cooling rack to remove them. Let sit at least two minutes before serving hot, warm, or at room temperature. Store leftovers in a well-sealed bag or storage container on the counter for up to 3 days or in the freezer for up to two weeks.

Cook's Notes:

If you'd like your muffins more quickly first thing in the morning— or at night-- mix the dry and wet ingredients separately the night before. Store the wet ingredients bowl in the fridge. Leave the dry ingredient mixture covered with plastic wrap or a plate and the greased muffin tin on the counter. Preheat the oven, stir together the two ingredient mixtures, add the berries, and you're on your way.

Pumpkin-Chocolate Chip Coffee Cup Muffins

makes 6 large (8 ounce) coffee cup muffins or 12 regular muffins

Every year in October, I begin making pumpkin bread and make it until the end of December. I make it for breakfasts, my choirs, to take to potlucks and for gifts. And while the bread is always obviously *my* pumpkin bread, each year finds me tweaking the recipe this way or that — a little maple syrup, a pinch of cardamom or cayenne — just to see what happens. A couple of years ago, I began to make all kinds of things in big, heavy, oven-safe mugs or cups (white French porcelain) because it was so much fun. If you don't have oven-safe mugs, you can make these muffins in tins, custard cups or ramekins. Rich, spicy and filling, they'll round out a meal of light soup like zucchini or turnip-pear. As a snack, they'll easily hold you over until the next meal.

1/3 cup softened butter plus extra for greasing cups or tins

1/4 cup dried cranberries

1/4 cup raisins

1/2 cup hot water

1/2 cup semi-sweet chocolate chips

1 2/3 plus 1/2 cup all-purpose white flour

1 cup canned pumpkin

2 eggs

1 1/4 cups sugar

1/3 cup milk

1/4 cup walnuts, chopped

1 teaspoon baking soda

1/4 teaspoon baking powder

3/4 teaspoon salt

3/4 teaspoon cinnamon

1/4 teaspoon nutmeg

1/2 teaspoon ground cloves

1 Preheat oven to 400° F. Grease cups or tins with extra softened butter.

2 Place cranberries, raisins and hot water in a small bowl; set aside.

3 In another small bowl, combine the chocolate chips and 1/2 cup flour; set aside.

4 Using an electric mixer (or by hand) beat together the softened 1/3 cup butter, pumpkin, eggs, sugar and milk.

5 Drain the cranberry-raisin mixture and add to the pumpkin mixture. Stir in the walnuts.

6 In a large bowl, combine 1 2/3 cups flour, baking soda baking powder, salt, cinnamon, nutmeg and cloves. Spoon the pumpkin mixture into the dry ingredients and mix until just blended. Fold in the floured chocolate chips.

7 Divide the batter between the prepared cups or tins. Bake 15-20 minutes until browned and just barely firm. Muffins are done when a toothpick stuck into the middle comes out almost clean. Let sit on a rack a minute or so before turning muffins onto the rack to cool completely. Or eat warm with butter or softened cream cheese mixed with honey.

Cook's Notes:

This batter also can be baked in a greased and floured 9x5-inch loaf pan. Bake at 350° F. 50-60 minutes or until toothpick comes out almost clean.

Savory Granola

For smooth soups needing a little crunch on top, try my savory granola. The herbs can be changed to suit the soup. For example, you could try basil and oregano with a tomato soup or sage with a fall squash soup. Serve in a small bowl at the table so guests can sprinkle on as little or as much as they like. Savory Granola also makes a healthy casserole or vegetable topping.

1   cup old-fashioned oats

1/4   teaspoon *each* kosher salt and fresh-ground pepper

1/8   teaspoon or a pinch Aleppo or crushed pepper

2   tablespoons finely grated Parmesan cheese

1/4   cup pecans or walnuts, finely chopped

1/4   teaspoon dried thyme

1/2   teaspoon dried rosemary, rubbed well between your hands or finely chopped

1   tablespoon olive oil

3   tablespoons vegetable broth

Preheat oven to 400° F. Mix all ingredients well in a medium bowl, then spread on a foil-lined baking sheet. Bake 20 minutes or until dry and crispy. Let cool on rack before scraping granola into a bowl.

Grilled Fish Spread

makes
1 cup

If you're having fish for supper, grill an extra fillet and use it to make this winner of a spread. For those living in Minnesota or Wisconsin, a well-seasoned walleye fillet makes this really special, but any grillable fish will work. Try salmon (add a bit of dill) or even catfish, depending on where you live.

6 ounces grilled fish

2 tablespoons lemon juice

1 tablespoon Dijon-style mustard

3 ounces cream or goat cheese, softened

2 tablespoons grated onion

2 tablespoons capers, chopped

Kosher salt and fresh-ground pepper

1/4 cup sharp cheese, such as Cheddar, minced (not grated)

1 In a medium bowl, chop or mash fish. Add other ingredients and mix well.

2 Taste and adjust seasonings. Serve on a platter surrounded by crackers or grilled bread.

Irish Soda Bread – American Style

makes 1 loaf or 10-12 slices

Traveling in Ireland, I found the morning soda bread a lovely, hearty whole-wheat loaf. There's nothing tastier or more warming than soda bread with a spread of butter and jam and a hot cup of tea. But this loaf, which uses all white flour, is the first "Irish" soda bread in my life and heart. It's closer to the soda bread Americans know and love, and I've no idea where the recipe came from — I've made it for 30 years or so. Occasionally it's a bit stubborn getting done all the way through, but be patient. It'll have a hard, crispy exterior and a tender, slightly sweet interior. If it's still a bit underdone in the center, slice and place the slices under the broiler or toast them, which is what I do the next day anyway. Serve this bread with Corned Beef and Potato Soup with Cheddar.

4 cups all-purpose flour

1/4 cup sugar

1 teaspoon salt

1 teaspoon baking powder

1/4 cup cold butter

1 1/2 cups buttermilk (for high-altitude baking, add 2-3 tablespoons more)

3 large eggs

1 1/2 cups currants or substitute raisins

1 teaspoon baking soda

1 Preheat oven to 375° F. Grease a 2-quart, round ovenproof bowl, casserole or deep cake pan.

2 In food processor or large mixing bowl, measure dry ingredients and mix well. Cut in the butter with blade attachment, knives or pastry blender.

3 In a large mixing cup, whisk together the buttermilk and eggs; add the currants and baking soda. Pour the liquid ingredients into the dry and mix well to form a very wet dough.

4 Turn the shaggy dough into the prepared baking bowl or pan and bake for about 1 hour until bread is very well-browned and firm in the center. Alternately, and for a more quickly-baked loaf, shape the dough into a rough round and bake it free-form on a greased, heavy baking sheet for an hour or so until crispy. A wooden skewer stuck in the middle of the bread should come out clean. If the bread isn't done, return it to oven for another 5 minutes and test again. You may have to test several times.

5 Let the loaf sit 15-20 minutes before cutting or it will crumble. Cool completely before wrapping tightly in foil and storing in the refrigerator. Will keep 3-4 days. Leftovers are excellent as is, but even better for toast made under the broiler. No jam needed.

Whole Wheat Rolls in the Bread Machine

12 large round rolls

My husband Dave's dad had a long-time friend and coworker named Bill Kalbus. Bill and his wife Annette retired to open a motel and restaurant in the mountains of Montana, and where they fed everyone from miles around for years. At home, Bill excelled at bread-machine baking in much smaller quantities. On one visit, we traveled high up into the hills to cook steaks on a fire. Bill gave me *only* the list of ingredients for these rolls, insisting I could just throw them all in the machine. It was up to me to work out how to do it. The result is this long-standing recipe well worth the time it takes to master it. I often make dozens of these rolls for church suppers, holidays or big events. There are never any left. The dough is only mixed in the bread machine, then taken out, shaped into rolls and baked in the oven. Instructions for altitude baking are included in the Cook's Notes. Bill and Annette are now baking goodies in those perfect ovens in the sky where there are no altitude or temperature problems. *Thanks, Bill.*

1   cup water

1/4   cup honey

2   tablespoons butter, softened, plus 1 tablespoon to melt for brushing rolls before baking

1   egg

1   teaspoon salt

1 1/4   cups whole-wheat flour

2   cups unbleached white flour

2   teaspoons yeast

1 Grease a 9x11-inch metal pan and set aside.

2 Add all ingredients to the bread machine container and start machine, using setting for *dough only*. This setting is to mix and rise the dough, but not to bake it. As the ingredients mix, you may need to add a little more water if the mixing blades are banging too loudly in the container.

3 When the cycle is over**, remove the dough from the machine and place on a floured board. Pat the dough into an oval and divide into thirds. Divide each third in half and in half again so you have 12 pieces of dough.

4 With floured hands, shape the 12 pieces into balls, pinching bottoms to create a round shape.

5 Place rolls, pinched side down and smooth side up, into the prepared pan.

6 Melt 1 tablespoon butter and lightly brush tops of rolls. Cover with plastic wrap and let rise until the rolls have filled the pan or just about doubled in size.

7 Preheat oven to 350° F. Bake rolls 15-20 minutes or until quite brown. For crispy rolls, remove from pan and cool on rack. For softer rolls, leave in pan to cool. Serve with butter and honey.

**At this point, you may place dough in a 1-gallon food storage bag, seal it well, except for one corner, and store the dough in the fridge for up to 2 days. When ready to bake, remove dough from refrigerator and continue at step 3.

Cook's Notes:

1.This dough also could be prepared in a standing electric mixer with a dough hook or by hand, but I find the bread machine the very best tool for mixing bread dough. 2. If you're baking at altitude (above 3,000 feet), you'll need to add an additional egg and quite a bit more water — 1/4 cup or more — to enable mixing. The dough also will rise more quickly due to lack of atmospheric pressure. 3. For a browner, heartier roll, add 1 tablespoon wheat germ with the flour.

Tuna Salad Quesadillas

makes 4 whole or 8 half quesadillas

Nearly everyone, including children, likes tuna salad sandwiches. Add to that, I've never met anyone who didn't like cheese quesadillas. Put them together — tuna salad and cheese grilled on a tortilla — and you'll have a favorite, quick and filling side for soup. You can use your own tuna salad recipe or try mine.

4   teaspoons butter

8   tortillas

2 2/3   cups tuna salad

4   slices Cheddar or Monterey Jack cheese

1 Preheat oven to 250° F. Put a baking sheet in the oven to warm.

2 For each quesadilla, melt 1 teaspoon butter in a medium skillet over medium heat. Add tortilla and top with about 1/3 cup tuna salad, spreading tuna evenly and leaving 1/2-inch space around the edge. Top with a slice of cheese and another tortilla.

3 Cook for 2 minutes or until toasted. Carefully turn and cook the other side until golden. Remove to the baking sheet in the oven to keep warm while you make the rest of the sandwiches.

4 Repeat with remaining three sandwiches. Serve hot.

Easy Tuna Salad

2   6-ounce cans tuna, drained, broken up with a fork

2   hard-cooked eggs, peeled and chopped

4   tablespoons mayonnaise (or to taste)

1   teaspoon Dijon-style mustard

1/2   teaspoon prepared horseradish, optional

1   tablespoon minced onion

1/3   cup *each* minced celery and minced dill pickles

Generous pinch *each* kosher salt, fresh-ground black pepper, crushed red pepper and dried dill.

1 In a medium bowl, mix all ingredients together well with a fork.

2 Taste and adjust for seasonings.

Garlic Bread
Grilled Tomato Sandwiches

makes 2 whole sandwiches or 4 halves

A young friend, visiting with his mother, asked this food blogger, "Tell me, how do you get a grilled cheese cooked nicely? No matter what I do, one side burns and the other side's got nada." I would guess that grilled cheese is the most-cooked sandwich in the United States and perhaps in a few other places where it's called, "cheese toast." Visiting the local bookstore lately, I noticed a whole book on grilled cheese. A whole book.

But come summer, I love a good grilled tomato sandwich. This version, made with thick and sturdy garlic bread, is at the top of my list. And, just like I told the kid who asked about the grilled cheese, I'll tell you to cook the sandwiches slowly rather than quickly. No flash frying allowed or the garlic will be burned and bitter. You'll need a sturdy bread or the sandwich will fall apart.

4 teaspoons each olive oil and butter	2 large, very thick slices of tomato (1/2-1 inch)
1 clove garlic, minced	Kosher salt and fresh ground pepper
4 slices good-sized rustic and crusty bread	2 teaspoons mayonnaise

1 Heat a large, heavy skillet over medium-low heat. Add olive oil, butter, and garlic and let cook together for 1 minute, swirling around to coat bottom of pan. Salt and pepper the sliced tomatoes.

2 Spread a little mayo on each piece of bread and then place two pieces plain side down in the buttered skillet. Add a tomato slice to each bread slice and top each with the last two slices of bread, plain side up.

3 Weigh the sandwich down with a grill press, foil-covered brick or even a small, heavy skillet.

4 Toast until golden, about 2-3 minutes; turn and toast the other side. Remove from skillet, slice sandwiches in half and serve hot.

Homemade Cheese or 2-1-2-1 Cheese

Makes 1 approximately 6-inch ball of fresh, firm cheese
or 1 cup soft, spreadable cheese

Making cheese like Brie or Manchego is an art form, and no one attempts making it without some serious study and/or apprenticeship. Not to mention the special equipment necessary for an endeavor like that. But simple, fresh cow's milk cheese that's made nearly in the time it takes to heat and drain the milk is something anyone can do and impress their friends all at the same time. "You made *cheese*?"

I call this 2-1-2-1 Cheese because after you've memorized the ingredients and the title, you'll make it without a recipe, knowing the proportions just from the name — perhaps much like farm wives and house wives did for years.

The idea for making this cheese came from Paris-based blogger, cookbook author, food-tour guide and pastry chef extraordinaire, David Lebovitz (davidlebovitz.com), who had a recipe on his blog for cheese made not with two cups of milk, but with two quarts. I either misread or was blind, but I made it my own way and have been doing so ever since. I'm beholden to David for many things — particularly for his witty, entertaining and instructive writing — including this recipe.

Read the recipe all the way through before beginning. While not difficult, it really helps to understand the process. You'll need plain white cheesecloth from the hardware or grocery store, as well as a colander or sieve and two pots or a pot and a bowl. Make sure you use whole milk and full-fat yogurt. You can eat the cheese immediately — soft and tender and lovely with honey or pepper. If you let it drain in the cloth a bit longer and refrigerate, you'll have a sliceable ball of cheese to make caprese salad or to serve with honey and thyme or fruit and bread.

2 cups whole milk

1 cup whole milk yogurt

2 teaspoons white vinegar (or lemon juice for a different flavor)

1 teaspoon salt

1 Place a bowl or pot in the sink (should be larger than the colander or sieve.) Set the colander inside the pot and line it with 3 or 4 layers of cheesecloth.

2 Mix all of the ingredients together in a medium saucepan over medium heat and bring to a gentle boil. Simmer 1-2 minutes or until you see some curds just beginning to form.

3 Pour the hot milk mixture carefully and slowly through the cloth-lined colander. Let drain 15 minutes for softer cheese or 30-45 minutes for a more firm cheese.

4 If you choose *soft*, spoon cheese into a bowl and either eat immediately as is (or topped with honey and pepper or fresh herbs) with crackers or bread or cover it well and refrigerate up to 2 days. If you choose *firm* cheese, gather up the corners of the cloth with the cheese in the middle and, twisting the cloth, squeeze out all of the liquid (whey) until you have a solid, firm cheese at the center. Repeat 2-3 times. The more you squeeze, the firmer and drier the cheese will be. Unwrap the cheese, disposing of the cheese cloth, and turn it out into a bowl for eating or storing, well covered, in the refrigerator for up to 2 days.

Cook's Notes:

Either cheese is lovely to eat as is, in omelets, on toast, with fruit, in lasagna, in caprese salad or on sandwiches. You can season the cheese as you like because this is your homemade cheese.

Faux Croque Monsieur or Ham-and-Cheese Grilled French Toast

serves 4

The real croque monsieur swims in a little sauce, as does the croque madame, albeit with the addition of a perfectly fried egg. My version takes the best of both and turns French Toast into a savory meal perfect for pairing with a light vegetable or bean soup without breaking the calorie budget. Choose good-quality ham and cheese; this is one of those "very few ingredients so they must all be excellent" recipes. Serve with hot soup, or add the fried egg and serve for breakfast.

2 tablespoons each butter and olive oil

2 eggs

1 tablespoon water

Salt and pepper

8 slices Italian bread

2 tablespoons Dijon-style mustard

1/2 pound Black Forest ham (or your favorite)

1/4 pound sliced Swiss cheese (I like Emmanthaler)

1 Preheat oven to 250 degrees° F., and place a cookie sheet in oven.

2 In a large skillet, heat oil and butter over medium heat. Beat eggs and water in large, shallow bowl (a pasta bowl works well). Season with a good-sized pinch of salt and pepper. Beat again.

3 Spread each piece of bread lightly with Dijon mustard. With the mustard-covered sides facing up, top four slices of bread with ham and cheese, dividing them equally among the four slices. Top with the remaining slices.

4 To prevent the sandwiches from becoming soggy, do just 2 at a time. Place one sandwich on a pancake turner and carefully lower into the beaten egg-water mixture. Carefully turn sandwich over (another pancake turner helps) and dip the other side well with the egg-water mixture. Repeat with another sandwich.

5 Gently place the two sandwiches in the heated pan. Cook until the first side is golden brown, 3-4 minutes. Turn over and cook the other side until brown. Remove to the cookie sheet in the oven to keep warm; repeat with the other two sandwiches.

Goat Cheese Spread with Dill and Red Onion

makes about 1 cup

Everyone likes cheese spread and nearly everyone likes goat cheese, which is available locally throughout the U.S. This spread adapts beautifully to whatever ingredients you have at hand. If you don't have dill, try thyme. Blend by hand or use a food processor. Delicious folded into an omelet or dolloped onto grilled salmon. And it tastes perfectly divine with a glass of Sancerre.

7 ounces goat cheese at room temperature

Pinch of kosher salt

1/4 teaspoon fresh-ground white or black pepper

2-4 tablespoons plain yogurt (start with 2 and add more, if needed)

1/4 cup chopped fresh dill, or more if desired

1 tablespoon finely minced red onion

1-2 drops hot sauce, optional

1 In a medium bowl, combine all ingredients except hot sauce and mash well with a table fork, adding more yogurt until cheese is very spreadable. Blend in hot sauce. Taste and adjust seasonings.

2 Serve with crackers or a sliced baguette — plain or grilled.

Meatloaf Panini with Dipping Sauce

makes 2 sandwiches

I was 20 before I ever ate a meatloaf sandwich. One afternoon I was at my friend Danny Izzo's house, and he asked if I'd like one. I've never looked back. One cold weekend night last year, I was casting around the kitchen for something different to do with a small amount of leftover meatloaf. If I don't want plain old cold meatloaf, I sometimes fry it up in pieces to have with eggs or crumble it with cheese into some pasta. That night, I just grabbed the grill pan and began to make what has since become one of our very favorite sandwiches of all time.

The meatloaf and cheese sandwiches are grilled on a grill pan or in a panini machine and served hot with either salsa or marinara for dipping. They're also tasty with no sauce at all. I've include a simple beef meatloaf recipe, as well as for my marinara, in case you don't have favorites.

4   slices whole-wheat bread

1   tablespoon butter

2   tablespoons coarse-ground or Dijon-style mustard

3-4   thin slices cooked meatloaf

4   slices Provolone or Cheddar cheese (Provolone for the marinara; Cheddar for the salsa)

1/4   cup fresh basil leaves

1/4   cup fresh spinach leaves

1   cup marinara or salsa for dipping

1 Heat the grilling pan or large cast-iron skillet over medium heat. Butter each slice of bread on one side. Spread mustard on the unbuttered side of 2 slices. Place 1 slice of bread, buttered side down, on the pan and layer with the meatloaf, cheese, basil and spinach leaves. Top with another slice of bread, buttered side up. Repeat for the other sandwich.

2 Place something heavy on top of the sandwiches such as a grill press, heavy pan or foil-covered brick, and grill until toasty brown on one side. Remove heavy object and turn the sandwiches over; grill until the second side is browned.

3 Serve hot with a ramekin of marinara or salsa on the side for dipping or dunking.

Easy Meatloaf:

1 pound ground meat (not too lean)	1/2 cup onion, minced
1 pound bulk breakfast sausage	2 slices bread, torn into pieces
4 cloves garlic, grated or finely minced	1/2 teaspoon fresh ground pepper
1 15-ounce can tomato sauce	1 teaspoon kosher salt
1 extra-large egg	1 tablespoon *each* dried basil and dried oregano
	1/4 cup beef broth

1 Preheat oven to 350° F. In a large bowl, lightly toss together with your hands all ingredients, except beef broth, until well combined. Pour in 1 tablespoon of broth at a time until the meat mixture holds together.

2 Turn meat mixture into a 9x5-inch loaf pan (I like glass for meatloaf) and bake for 1 hour or until loaf is nicely browned on top and just firm to the touch. Holding the pan with hot pads or oven mitts, very carefully pour off any fat. Let meatloaf remain in pan, covered with foil, for 10-15 minutes before slicing and serving.

Easy Marinara:

makes about 3 1/2 cups marinara sauce

2 tablespoons olive oil or butter	28-ounce can Italian tomatoes (I like Cento), chopped
1/4 teaspoon fresh-ground black pepper	1/2 teaspoon *each* dried basil and oregano
1/3 cup onion, minced	2 tablespoons fresh parsley, minced
1 stalk celery, minced	1-inch piece Parmesan or a small Parmesan rind
1 tablespoon carrot, minced	Pinch *each* of kosher salt, sugar and ground cayenne
1 clove garlic, minced	

1 In a 2-quart sauce pan, heat the oil or butter and black pepper over medium heat; add the onion, celery and carrot. Saute, stirring often, until softened, about 5 minutes. Add garlic during the last minute or so.

2 Stir in tomatoes, basil, oregano, parsley and Parmesan and bring to a boil. Reduce heat to a simmer and let cook 15 minutes, stirring regularly. Taste and season with salt, sugar and cayenne.

Desserts

While I love to bake or make big desserts as much as the next cook, I find I truly adore the very quick, healthy and/or simple desserts we can eat on a nearly daily basis — a square of dark chocolate, a spoonful of yogurt over fruit. I also know that when I'm having friends to dinner or cooking for a party, I don't always have time to make a fancy dessert, but I love being able to sit and relax after a meal. Between work, straightening the house, setting the table, getting the wine ready and cooking the meal, where's the time for the tart? Still, everyone remembers the sweet! So I put together this group of fast and fun desserts. Some are warm drinks with a bit of a kick. Others are microwaved chocolate decadence or baby pumpkin "pies" done in under a minute — make them alone or with any kiddoes in the house. There are also ideas for sweet, icy parfaits using ice cream, fresh fruit, liqueur and crumbled store-bought shortbread.

But first,

Here's a list of nearly-instant desserts you only need to plate, serve or pour with no sweat at all:

Dessert wine:

Tell the wine shop what you're serving for dinner and just offer a great dessert wine for dessert. Buy some swanky glasses and enjoy saving calories.

Port, brandy, Armagnac, etc.:

Keep a good bottle of one of these excellent digestifs and share it with your friends. No one drinks much, so it'll last a while. Antique stores often have gorgeous port glasses or snifters. Indulge. A little blue cheese or walnuts with port is a wonderful thing.

Frou-frou coffees:

Make decaf cappuccino, mochas, or lattes. Who needs more??

Affogato:

This Italian dessert consists of nothing more than espresso poured over vanilla ice cream or gelato. Regular American coffee works, too. Add Amaretto or Grand Marnier, if you like. No espresso maker? Buy some a few shots of espresso at the local coffee shop and store in the fridge.

Plain coffee with a kick:

Add a generous splash of brandy à la Irish coffee to put the last kiss on a winter evening.

Chocolates:

Visit a wonderful chocolate shop and buy a one-pound assorted box or a big, thin bar to share. Serve with hot coffee, a big red wine or a little brandy.

Caramels:

If your grandma or aunt makes caramels at Christmas, get them to make extra for you and freeze them.

Warmed or spiced nuts:

Just a healthy, happy crunch at the end of the meal.

Cheese:

Be French. Add a cheese tray to the end of your meal. No need for crackers. Serve 3 or 4 different cheeses: a goat, a blue, a sheep, and a basic that everyone will eat, such as an aged Gouda or a Cheddar. Many shops have local cheeses that are a treat to buy. Look up the cheese makers on the Internet and print out a little blurb for each cheese.

Bakery-purchased pound or angel cake:

Serve slices piled with fresh berries, sliced peaches and/or whipped cream. Freeze blueberries in the summer and enjoy them come February like this.

Upscale ice cream bars:

People love them, but don't buy them. However, they will eat yours.

Fresh fruit in season:

If you cut it, they will come. Garnish with a little fresh mint, if you have some.

Scottish shortbread drizzled with melted chocolate:

Serve with hot tea laced with brandy.

Instant Ice Cream Desserts

These delightful options for favorite ice cream flavors really are instant!

Vanilla

Top with crushed peppermints and drizzle with chocolate sauce

Add sliced apples sautéed in butter and cinnamon sugar

Layer with crushed Thin Mints and drizzle with Crème de Menthe

Grill apricots, chop and mix into ice cream with honey and walnuts

À la Patalano (good cooking friends of mine): Pour heavy cream over ice cream

Strawberry

In a parfait glass, layer the ice cream, fresh sliced peaches, Amaretto, candied ginger and crushed shortbread or butter cookies

Soften and stir in mini-chocolate chips

Put a softened spoonful plus a banana slice between two vanilla wafers. Roll in grated chocolate. Wrap individually and freeze.

Raspberry sorbet

Add to a large wine glass and top with fresh raspberries and lots of sparkling wine

Chocolate

Put one scoop in a beer mug and top with stout

Put one scoop in small mug and pour in Bailey's Irish Cream and/or coffee

Soften ice cream and spread between a waffle you've cut in half. Wrap and freeze.

Ginger or Cinnamon

Cut a peach in half, grill, slice and spoon over ice cream.

Layer in a tall glass with cake pieces, fruit topping and whipped cream

Fresh Fruit Ice Cream Toppers

serves
4-6

Have extra fruit? Cook it up to spoon over ice cream.

In a 3-quart saucepan, place 3-4 cups fresh, fruit — blueberries, rhubarb, peaches, etc. — along with about 1/4 cup -1/3 cup sugar and a cup of water. Use a bit more sugar for rhubarb and taste any fruit to see if you need more or less sweetening. If you like cinnamon, add a pinch for extra flavor. You could also add a cinnamon stick or a little vanilla. For blueberries, I add about 1/2 teaspoon grated lemon to the mixture. Over medium heat, bring the fruit, water, sugar and flavoring to a boil. Turn down heat and simmer, stirring often, until thickened to the texture you desire. Add a little water if needed. Serve hot or cold over ice cream. Make ahead and refrigerate 1-2 days.

Individual Microwaved Chocolate Pudding Cakes

serves 4-5

Chocolate — dark chocolate — in small, loving, quick doses is exactly what the doctor ordered. Easy for a Valentine's dessert or for late-night desires, these tiny sweets are just big enough to satisfy that chocolate craving without going overboard. Use all coffee for an alcohol-free pudding cake or decaf if eating them late at night.

6-ounces good-quality bittersweet chocolate, chopped

1/2-pound (2 sticks) salted butter, cut into 1-inch pieces

1/4 cup strong coffee

1/4 cup brandy

1/2 cup brown sugar

4 eggs, beaten

Whipped cream, crème fraiche with cocoa, fresh berries for garnish, optional

1 Place chopped chocolate in a large bowl and set aside. Heat butter, coffee, brandy and brown sugar in a small saucepan over medium heat until the mixture just begins to boil. Pour coffee mixture over chocolate, cover with a large plate for 2-3 minutes, then stir until chocolate is melted and mixture is smooth. Whisk in eggs until well-combined.

2 Place pieces of parchment paper, cut to fit, into the bottom of 4 or 5 microwave-safe ramekins or cups. Divide chocolate mixture evenly among the ramekins, filling them no more than half full. Cook each ramekin separately in microwave at full power for 30-60 seconds, checking at 30 seconds and adding 5 seconds at a time until pudding is barely set. Repeat with remaining ramekins until all puddings are cooked. Let cool a least a few minutes before serving either warm or at room temperature. Puddings can be cooled completely, covered and stored in the refrigerator a day ahead. This dessert can be softer or firmer, depending on your tastes and how long you cook it. Garnish as desired with whipped cream, crème fraîche dusted with cocoa powder, a drizzle of half-and-half or fresh berries.

Cook's Note: Microwaves vary a bit; you may need to try one pudding first to see how long your oven will take to make these desserts.

Pumpkin Custard
with Cinnamon Crème Fraîche

serves
4-5

One Thanksgiving, I had too much pumpkin pie filling, which went into the fridge for another day. I began to play around with cooking it in custard cups. Not-too-sweet, but spicy, these pumpkin custards taste like your favorite pumpkin pie, minus the crust. Whisked together and microwaved individually in about a minute each, they make a warm ending to simple or elegant meals and will become a part of your year-round cooking repertoire. If there are kids around, let them help. Leftovers make perfect fall breakfasts with a spoonful of plain yogurt. No ramekins? Make them in microwave-safe coffee cups.

Butter, softened, for greasing
   ramekins or custard

1 egg, beaten

1 1/4 cups canned pumpkin
      (substitute canned mashed
      sweet potatoes or mashed
      fresh acorn squash)

1/2 cup white sugar

1/4 teaspoon salt

1 teaspoon ground cinnamon,
   plus extra for garnish

1/4 teaspoon ground ginger

1/4 teaspoon ground cloves

1 1/4 cups nonfat evaporated
      milk or half-and-half

2-3 tablespoons crème
     fraîche or whipping
     cream, for garnish

1 Grease with butter or cooking spray 4 – 5 microwave safe ramekins.

2 Whisk the rest of the ingredients, except crème fraîche, together and, dividing evenly, pour filling into ramekins until 2/3 full.

3 Cook each ramekin in the microwave on full power for 1 minute. If custard begins to overflow, stop microwave and let cool a few seconds before continuing, cooking until custard is nearly firm. You might also try cooking at 50 percent power for a little longer. Using mitts or potholders, remove from microwave and repeat until all ramekins have been cooked. Don't overcook. Custard is done when nearly firm, but still moves a bit when jiggled. Let cool for a few minutes and top with a teaspoon of crème fraîche or whipped cream. Dust with a sprinkle of cinnamon for garnish.

Cook's Notes: Microwaves vary. You may need to cook a trial custard first to decide on the best power level/cooking time for your microwave. Another option is to fill the ramekins only half full to avoid spillovers. To bake in the oven, preheat to 350° F. Bake 30 minutes or until set.

Very Fast Maple Syrup Brown Rice Pudding

4 servings

I once had a hankering for rice pudding, but didn't feel like going to the trouble of cooking it stovetop or in the oven. Just for a laugh, I decided to try an individual microwaved version — and I've been making it ever since. My husband swoons over this dessert, and it couldn't be simpler. What's not to like about cream and maple syrup? If you bring home leftover take-out rice, this is a great use for it. If you make it for company, and they don't see you stick the bowls in the microwave, they'll never know it didn't take an hour.

2 cups cooked brown rice, preferably leftover, cold and somewhat dry

1 cup heavy cream

1/4 cup real maple syrup

For each serving, spoon ½ cup cooked brown rice into a small, microwave-safe dessert bowl. Over the rice, pour about 1/4 cup heavy cream. Microwave on high power 45-60 seconds.* Using mitts, remove from the oven. Pouring carefully, make a generous puddle of maple syrup in the middle of the hot, creamy rice. Eat immediately. And happily, I might add.

*Microwaves vary. You might want to cook a trial rice pudding first.

Cook's Notes: I'm particularly fond of Minnesota maple syrup, but any good-quality syrup will do.

Simply Excellent Strawberry Shortcake from Scratch (or Not)

8 servings

8 freshly baked or purchased sweetened biscuits or shortcakes, sliced in half

1/2 cup best-quality raspberry jam, at room temperature

1 1/2 quarts in-season, ripe strawberries, hulled and sliced

1/2 quart in-season, ripe strawberries, hulled, and mashed well with 1 tablespoon sugar

1 1/2 quarts homemade vanilla ice cream

1 cup whipped cream

Spread all the shortcake halves with jam. Place one-half shortcake in a cereal or soup bowl, jam side up, and top with plain sliced strawberries and whipped cream. Add the other shortcake half and repeat. Garnish with the sweetened strawberry slices and add a scoop of vanilla ice cream on the side. Repeat with other seven servings.

Cook's Notes:

I like Marion Cunningham's shortcake recipe from her baking book, but purchased pound cake works well here, too. Make the ice cream yourself if you have time.

Kiwi "Tarts" with Gingersnap Crust

4 servings

I'd never been a big kiwi fan (it's the brown, fuzzy thing), but one fall when they were cheap and gorgeous — the produce department had sliced open a couple to try – I brought some home. I brought too many home. Since custards and any vanilla puddings are some of my husband's favorite desserts, I decided to make a simple pastry cream (basically a vanilla pudding) and add a few slices of kiwi on the top. In the end, I put a small, thin gingersnap on the bottom of the cup to add a bit of spice and crunch. Best made just before serving, you can, if you need to, make them the morning you'll need them. Just brush the kiwi with a little heated apricot jam before storing, uncovered, in the refrigerator for a few hours.

Pastry Cream:

2 cups whole milk

1 egg yolk

1/3 cup white sugar

2 1/2 tablespoons cornstarch

2 tablespoons unsalted butter

1/8 teaspoon salt

1 1/2 teaspoons vanilla extract

Tarts:

4 thin, store-bought gingersnap cookies

12 slices kiwi, peeled (3-4 kiwi)

1 tablespoon apricot jam, warmed

1 Combine milk, egg yolk, sugar and cornstarch in a heavy saucepan. Cook over low heat, stirring often, until the mixture boils. Remove from heat and stir in butter, salt and vanilla. Cook for 2-3 minutes.

2 Place 1 gingersnap in the bottom each of 4 ramekins or custard cups, and spoon pastry cream on top, dividing evenly. (You may have a little leftover for a snack.) After a few minutes, stand three slices of kiwi upright in each tart and, if storing in the fridge, brush with the warmed apricot jam. Otherwise, serve immediately.

Cocoa with a Kick (or Not)

Adults usually will not admit they love cocoa, but if someone makes it for them, they're delighted. Skip the typical dessert or coffee and make a warming pot of cocoa for your friends or family. Adults will enjoy choosing a dash of liqueur for their cup, and everyone will like squirting in real whipped cream and sprinkling it with cinnamon or cocoa powder. Fresh cocoa is best, but you can also make it ahead and store it in a carafe for an hour or two.

Or why not serve cocoa hot, in small bowls with a scoop of vanilla, almond, peppermint or chocolate ice cream? The cocoa, of course, melts the ice cream, but if you're quick, you can get a cool spoonful. If you'd rather drink hot chocolate, directions are in the Cook's Notes.

6 cups (48 ounces) whole milk

1/3 cup granulated sugar

1/4 cup Dutch-process cocoa

Pinch of salt

Amaretto, brandy, peppermint schnapps or other liqueur

Whipped cream sweetened with sugar and flavored vanilla extract

Heat milk over medium heat; do not allow to boil. In the meantime, mix together sugar, cocoa and salt. When milk is steaming, whisk in cocoa mixture until well-blended. If desired, pour 1-2 tablespoons liqueur into each cup. Top with sweetened, vanilla whipped cream. Serve hot.

Cook's Notes:

If you'd like a cocoa mix, try Penzey's (800-741-7787); it's delicious, with a hint of cinnamon. The mix comes in a variety of sizes, as well as a gift jar.

For 1 serving of hot chocolate: Grate 1-2 ounces good-quality semi-, bittersweet or milk chocolate into 8 ounces very warm (not boiling), milk, which can be sweetened with 1/4 teaspoon sugar. Whisk together milk, chocolate and 1/4 teaspoon vanilla extract. No problem if you'd like to mix chocolates; they're all good together with milk. Adjust proportions to your taste.

Cranberry-Ginger Bread Pudding

4 servings

During November or December when fresh cranberries are in season, you might find yourself with a few berries left over from making cranberry bread or sauce. I like to keep a spare pound or two in the freezer for use throughout the winter. For this bread pudding, muffins or pancakes, chop them frozen and stir them in. There's little else like bread pudding — it comes together quickly and will make family and guests quite happy. The recipe easily halves or doubles as needed and makes a delightful breakfast, as well as dessert since it's not overly sweet. Add 1/2 teaspoon candied ginger to one layer for a spicier pudding.

6 teaspoons butter, softened

8 slices baguette, torn into about 4 pieces each

8 tablespoons chopped fresh or frozen cranberries (substitute dried cranberries)

4 tablespoon raisins

1-2 Granny Smith or other tart apples cored, unpeeled and sliced thinly into 16 slices

Cinnamon

4 eggs, beaten together

2 cups milk

1/2 teaspoon vanilla

1/2 teaspoon ground ginger

1/4 cup granulated sugar

4 teaspoons grated or finely chopped white chocolate, optional

Preheat oven to 400° F.

1 With 2 teaspoons of the butter, grease 4 large ramekins or oven-safe coffee cups and place on a rimmed baking sheet.

2 Fit four pieces of bread into each ramekin, overlapping to fit. Add 1 tablespoon cranberries, a few raisins, and 2 slices of apple. Sprinkle lightly with cinnamon. Repeat layers three times.

3 Beat together remaining ingredients, except white chocolate. Dividing evenly, pour over the bread mixture. Don't fill cups more than 3/4 full. With clean fingers, gently press the top pieces of bread down into the custard mixture to moisten them. Dot the top of each pudding with about a teaspoon of butter.

4 Bake 30-40 minutes or until golden and the custard mixture is barely set.

5 Remove from oven, top with white chocolate, if using. Cool on wire rack at least 10 minutes before serving.

Virgin Blond(i)es

makes about 20 blondies

When I first began food blogging, I went on a jag baking blonde brownies. After baking batch after batch of sweets and sharing them with neighbors — which I adored doing — I decided MY blonde brownies needed their own name, so I dubbed them "Virgin Blond(i)es". From measuring to pulling them out of the oven, it only takes about 35 minutes to whip up a batch. They also freeze easily — thaw them unwrapped. For non-virgin blondies, make the chocolate version.

1-2 tablespoons butter, softened

1/2 cup unsalted peanuts, chopped

8 tablespoons (4 ounces) unsalted butter, melted

1/2 cup peanut butter, chunky or smooth

2 large eggs, beaten together

3/4 cup brown sugar

3/4 cup granulated sugar

1 tablespoon vanilla extract

1 teaspoon almond extract

1 1/2 cups all-purpose flour

1 teaspoon baking powder

1/2 teaspoon salt

1 cup peanut butter, butterscotch or chocolate chips

1 Preheat oven to 350° F. With the softened butter, grease a 9"x13"x2" metal baking pan and set aside. Toast nuts in a small skillet over low heat for five minutes, stirring regularly. Set aside.

2 In a large mixing bowl, combine melted butter and peanut butter until smooth. Beat in eggs, sugars and extracts. In a separate bowl, stir together the dry ingredients — flour, baking powder and salt. Slowly add the dry ingredients to the butter mixture, beating until just well-mixed. Fold in chips and nuts. With a rubber spatula, spread dough into prepared pan and smooth top of batter.

3 Bake 20-25 minutes or until barely golden brown at corners and light golden brown at center. Cool completely on wire rack. Cut into squares and serve. Store tightly covered at room temperature.

Grilled Peaches or Figs with Cheese, Honey, Thyme and Black Pepper

4 servings

Perfect for that hot summer night or early fall evening when dessert calls, but it's just too hot for the oven. Choose peaches or figs that are fairly ripe, but still firm. The grilled fruit is delicious on its own, just drizzled with honey and dusted with black pepper. Or serve them with a scoop of ice cream.

Canola oil

2 large peaches or 8 fresh figs, cleaned, cut in half and pitted

4 ounces goat or blue cheese, softened

2 teaspoons honey

2 teaspoons fresh thyme

Fresh-ground black pepper

Preheat clean grill to medium-high. Brush pitted, halved peaches or figs with a little bit of canola oil and place cut-side down on the grill. Watching carefully, let cook 3-4 minutes for peaches and 2-3 minutes for figs, turning them over when grill marks are well established, but not too blackened. Cook another 2 minutes (peaches) or 1 minute (figs) until tops of cut sides begin to dry slightly. Remove from grill and cool briefly. In small bowls, top each peach half or two fig halves with 2 tablespoons cheese (goat for peaches; blue for figs), drizzle with honey, sprinkle with thyme leaves and a grind or two of black pepper.

One-Minute Apple Crisp

serves 1

1/2 teaspoon cold butter

1 large apple such as Honeycrisp

1/8 teaspoon cinnamon

1/2 teaspoon sugar

Pinch of nutmeg

2 tablespoons granola

1 Place butter in a large, microwave-safe coffee cup or ramekin. Microwave on high about 5 seconds or until the butter is softened, but not necessarily melted. Brush part of the butter around the inside of the cup. Put the brush, which will still have a little butter on it, aside.

2 Slice a "cheek" — or two — off the apple, leaving the peel on. Use a sharp, thin knife to cut the apple into 10-12 very thin slices. Place the apple slices in the cup and brush and stir them with the buttered brush. Top with cinnamon, sugar, and nutmeg. Sprinkle apples with granola.

3 Cover with a small, microwave-safe plate, and microwave at full power for 1 minute. Remove carefully from microwave, uncover and eat while warm.

Acknowledgements

No one does this alone. My team included Patricia Miller, editor; Amanda Weber, designer; Drew Robinson, CS (sommelier); and Daniel Craig, artist. These folks worked with a rookie author, mostly for soup. They made it happen and turned a previously solo experience into a fun team effort. Writing any book, even a small one, can be lonely. Not with these folks on board. Thank you, friends, thank you.

Legendary Thai blogger, Leela Punyaratabandhu (shesimmers. com), gave special help in creating my Thai soup. The New York Times food writer and cookbook author Melissa Clark (lucky for me, married to Dave's cousin, Daniel) graciously gave me the go-ahead to use the basis for one of her most tasty dip recipes to create Spicy Cucumber with Feta Soup. Melissa is also the person who, five years ago, said, "Write a blog first. Then see about a book." She was, as always, spot on. St. Paul award-winning author, David Robinson, coached me about the publishing process and served as a wonderfully successful model.

I also thank with a grateful heart several friends who wouldn't let me give up. "How's the book coming?" was their mantra. Pastor Chris Kliesen Wehrman, Roberta Kagin, Sue Hall, Lani Jordan, Kim Craig, Margo Dickinson, Jeanne and Tony Patalano, and Helen Barrionuevo were part of the group who just knew I could do it. Rick Lester really believed I could cook, wine, dine and change the world. My blog readers, now numbering over 71,000, willingly put up with many, many soups. I really appreciate these readers for being my audience and faithful listeners all these years.

No one grows old at the table.   ...Italian Proverb

Thank you to the wonderful testers for this book. We had fun cooking, tasting and drinking wine together!

Paula Mielke

Prospect Park
    United Methodist Choir

Lani Jordan + Tom Harm

Sue Hall

Kim + Dan Craig

John Gregory Grooms

Margo + Mark Dickinson

Dave Morgan

Sean Morgan

Mary Pat Garman

Simon Penner

Sara Hillman

Sandy + Rick Lester

Helen Barrionuevo

Drew + Jill Robinson

Patricia Miller

Bonnie Parent

Deb Van de Weghe

John Grooms

Chris Kliesen-Wehrman
    and David Nyberg

Sarah + Chris Wilkerson

Loren Palmer

Joyce Smith

Bonnie Bassett

Jan Wilson

Liz Richards

Leighton Holmes

Meg + Don Arnosti

Jim Kellison + Friends

Debbie + Paul Zisla

Jan Keder

This baby of mine wouldn't have been conceived, hatched or born without my chief bottle washer (He did actually wash most of the dishes for this book, although he got lunch and/or dinner in the bargain.) and best dinner companion, husband David Morgan. He mostly paid the bills for the groceries and never complained, even when he ate the same thing in many versions or saw me buy just one more kind of soup bowl. He even learned to make soup himself. I Love You.

Index

Made in the USA
Lexington, KY
29 September 2014